Twelfth Edition

A CHANGING CALIFORNIA

Jack Carney

CONSENSUS PUBLISHERS

Editor: John A. Bradley

A CHANGING CALIFORNIA, Twelfth Edition

2007 Jack Carney. All Rights Reserved

Printed in the United States of America
For information address Consensus Publishers,

9869 Karmont Avenue, South Gate, CA 90280

Fax: (562) 806-2633

ISBN 1-879861-50x6

To
Natalya Edith Alcerro
and
Catherine Maeve Sheehan

TABLE OF CONTENTS—AND PRINCIPAL TOPICS

Preface

Having completed the writing of this twelfth edition of A *Changing California,* I again renew my original hopes for my efforts--that my work helps readers gain a considerably more substantial understanding of the governance of the most change-oriented community in the world, how it came into being, and how it is changing. Like its earlier versions this twelfth edition is particularly a brief but comprehensive description of the important prevailing circumstances, problems, structures, and functions of California politics and government.

Happily, with the sometimes arduous task of bringing a new edition of a book into existence comes the felicitous opportunity to thank those who inspired or assisted. I specially thank here Joe Dana, founder and first President of Consensus Publishers, Inc., John A. Bradley, who edited my entire manuscript, and all who reviewed my work. Particular thanks to Professor Mike Kennedy. And for those who in other ways encouraged my efforts I am grateful: Angela Ianni, Bruce Unruh, Edgar F. Love, Jim O'Grady, Gunther Alcerro, and Seán E. Carney. I also acknowledge my debt to all from whose research and writing I have drawn, but any error of fact or opinion is my own.

Jack Carney

Introduction:
American Conquest of California

Before 1846, several American presidents sought to buy Mexico's Province of California.* Mexico refused to sell. In 1846, President James Polk, who himself tried to buy California, decided on war.**

Regardless of political opposition,***in 1846, Polk sent a force under General Stephen Watts Kearny into thinly populated California. Governor Pío Pico mounted a fierce resistance. In December, Don Pío's brother, Andrés, leading a civilian force of Californians, intercepted the invading U.S. Army Dragoons at San Pascual, northeast of San Diego, and inflicted a crushing defeat. But after San Pascual, outnumbered and vastly outgunned, California resistance weakened and collapsed.

After losing in California, Mexico still refused to sell the Province of California. President Polk then decided on an expanded war on Mexico's center of power in southern Mexico.

There were four major battles in the war – all of them south of California. The U.S. won all four. Mexico lacked sufficient artillery and ammunition. Tragically, the seizing and holding of California for the U.S. meant that an estimated 40,000 Mexicans were to die.****Lamentably, U.S. deaths exceeded 13,000. Mostly, the American dead were poor, and risked their lives for $7.00 per month.

---

*The Province of California, also called Upper California or *Alta* California, included nearly all of the area of the Mexican Cession of 1848, ending the U.S.-Mexico War. (See map on p.i x).

**Polk made his fortune on slavery. He wanted California for more slave territory (plan defeated in the state of California by California's state government almost immediately).

***Among those opposing the U.S.-Mexico War over California was Abraham Lincoln (later president). John Quincy Adams (former president) also opposed the war, as did Ulysses S. Grant (future president).

****Estimate by Abiel Livermore, *The War with Mexico Revisited*. (Boston: American Peace Society, 1850).

The Sale

The war over, the U.S. pushed the sale of California for $15 million, about five cents per acre. Mexico feared that if it did not capitulate to the sale, the U.S. would take still more of Mexico.*

The American State of California was by far the most important part of the Mexican Cession. The Cession also included the present States of Nevada and Utah, most of Arizona and New Mexico, and parts of Colorado, Texas, and Wyoming.

*The U.S. did not want to take populous southern Mexico in 1848. It did not want to fight a long guerrilla war there.

X
Nativism* - Then and Now

The dominant (and Nativist) U.S. Army officer corps was, during the U.S. –Mexican War, beating some of their soldiers and prisoners with rawhide and branding them with cattle branding irons.**It was in this climate that over 5,300 regular army soldiers who saw duty in the War deserted.

After the Civil War Nativism receded.***But it was evident in the passage of Proposition 187 in 1994(See p.17.), in current extreme proposals to rid the country of undocumented, and measures outlawing affirmative action and bilingual education.

---

*Nativism is a policy of esteeming native inhabitants over immigrants.

**The U.S. (in 1861), banned the army's use of rawhide beatings. In the Civil War both General Grant and Lee discouraged brandings (banned in 1871).

***We began the long process of discarding our historic prejudices. Finally, while the American people and government were imperialist in the 1840s (believers in Manifest Destiny-expansion to the Pacific), today the American people are not imperialist.

Part I
California's
Changing
Constitution

The endless tide of immigration and the forced-draft growth of California's economy have made it a kaleidoscope succession of states, changing from year to year, almost from day to day.

Gladwin Hill

1 CHAPTER
= STATE OF CALIFORNIA'S CONSTITUTIONAL SCHEME

LEGACIES OF THE CALIFORNIA INDIANS

Indians, of course, discovered California and America. The California Indians, here for perhaps 15,000 years, lived under Spanish law (1769-1822) and loose Mexican rule (1822-1846). They constituted the bulk of California's population (about 150,000) at the beginning of the U.S. - Mexican War (1846).

But under American military rule (1846-1849) and early California state rule (beginning in 1849) their number was vastly reduced. This was not only because of disease, but by reason of being subjected to onerous abuses.

By 1860, about 10 years after statehood, the Indian population plunged from about 150,000 to about 30,000. U.C.L.A. historian John Caughey described this as "heartless liquidation."[1] Totally submerged, the California Indians did not influence the development of California's constitutional schemes.

Today, due to the generosity of California voters giving the California Indians a virtual monopoly of casino gambling by passing Proposition 1-A, they are rescued from being completely powerless politically. With less that 1/2 of 1 percent of California's population, by the early 2000s, they became the most powerful lobby in California, and the biggest contributors to political campaigns. Though not responsible for the crimes of their forebears, the voters have taken giant steps to remedy historic wrongdoings.

1. John W. Caughey, California. (Englewood Cliffs, N.J.: Prentice-Hall, Inc., 1953) p. 339

SPANISH AND MEXICAN HERITAGES

Spanish exploration of the coastal area above Mexico began in 1542, when an expedition led by Juan Cabrillo "discovered" San Diego Bay. Myriad expeditions followed, but not until 1769, when Gaspar de Portolá and Fray Junípero Serra established a mission and a fort at the current *situs* of San Diego, did Spanish occupation become actuality. Spain was trying to block Russian and British expansion.

The Spanish Franciscan Fathers eventually constructed 21 *missions*, the northernmost at Sonoma, to train and preserve the Indians, who were to be a basic element of the society. *Presidios* (forts) were built to secure the missions (which were agricultural *pueblos* [towns] as well as churches), and separate pueblos sprang up along the mission trails. These institutions were the beginnings of many California cities.

The Spanish era ended in 1822, when Mexico (after winning independence from Spain in 1821) began to rule California. Between 1834 and 1846, it secularized the missions, thus essentially ending the Franciscan design, and in the so-called Laws of 1837, provided a government for California, with a governor appointed by the central government in Mexico City, a popularly elected seven member legislature, and a judicial structure similar to our present one, but with the *alcalde* — a composite of local judge, mayor, and chief of police — the dominant figure.

Though Mexican rule brought to California concepts of *republicanism, representation,* and *constitutionalism,* both our Mexican and Spanish heritages are (like our Indian), principally in areas other than government. For instance, Spanish language place names survive, the local vocabulary has been influenced, and certain trends in the architecture and furniture of the Mexican era persist, as does the cuisine. Also, land titles rest on Spanish and Mexican bases, and California community property laws are founded on Spanish law.

LEGACY OF THE AMERICAN PERIOD (1846-1849)

The so-called American period, inaugurated early in the

general war with Mexico (1846-1848), when the annexation of California was declared by President James Polk, conveyed a meaningful legacy: resentment by Americans arriving during American military rule, of the incongruent *alcalde* governance. Carried over from the Mexican period, it violated the principle of separation of powers, a custom these Americans already cherished, and increasingly enshrined. Not surprisingly, the California Constitution (unlike the U.S. Constitution) includes a specific statement of separation of governmental powers.

LEGACIES OF THE AMERICAN STATE CONSTITUTIONS AND THE U.S. CONSTITUTION

Inexperienced in lawmaking the framers relied chiefly on the constitution of Iowa — most modern in the West — and to a lesser extent on New York's recently revised constitution. Also, the weight of other state constitutions, as well as of the U.S. Constitution, may be seen. It incorporated the entire federal Bill of Rights.

CALIFORNIA'S FIRST CONSTITUTION (1849)

Certain good may be said of the first Constitution. It was a simple and clear statement of basic principles and procedures, and popular approval was overwhelming — 12,872 for, 811 against. Even Congress did not derogate it, though complaining about methods followed — particularly the call to the convention, and the fashioning of a state instead of a territorial government (which went into effect immediately, before admission to statehood — mostly to check lawlessness). But eventually it was criticized for not limiting the Legislature's power to tax and spend, and because under it taxes had become "unduly high" and corporations exercised "too much control" over California's government, particularly the Legislature.

The 1849 Constitution was replaced not so much because it was a flawed document, but owing to severe economic and social troubles of the 1870's. Long past were the lush days of the gold rush; the Comstock Lode (mostly silver) had begun its final decline. Unemployment climbed as thousands of Chinese railroad workers entered (upon completion of the transcontinental railroad in 1869). In one year, a record 22,000 arrived in San Francisco alone.

DENIS KEARNEY AND CALIFORNIA'S PRESENT CONSTITUTION (1879)

In the late 1870's, workers flocked to the newly organized Kearneyite (Workingmen's) Party. Headed by Denis Kearney, a County Cork, Ireland immigrant, it opposed private importation of cheap alien labor, corruption in government, dishonest banking,

Denis Kearney. All his speeches conveyed this message: The capitalists must create jobs for the workers.

plutocratic control of California by corporations, and land monopoly.* It demanded constitutional change. As the depression of the 1870's worsened, farmers (suffering particularly from the monopolistic methods of banks, big landowners, and railroads) joined the Kearneyites' clamor for reform. In 1877, a call for a constitutional convention was approved by the voters.

Kearney's specific program was hardly radical by today's standards. But Kearney's fiery rhetoric, and his recommendation that "Every workingman should get a musket," frightened conservatives, much as Shays's Rebellion had alarmed the Founding Fathers of the U.S. Constitution.

Fearing the Kearneyites might control the convention, Democrats and Republicans dropped their labels and became "Nonpartisans." In a further design, conservatives got an additional 32 delegates-at-large seats added to the convention. All were won by Nonpartisans. By then, every newspaper in the state was opposing Kearney.

Of the 152 convention delegates, 51 were Workingmen. Eleven were Republicans, ten Democrats, two Independents, and 78 Nonpartisan. Most (57) were lawyers or farmers (39).

The draft constitution restricted the Legislature, particularly in finance; exposed corporations to much more severe regulation; and directed the Legislature to deter Chinese immigration.

Clearly, the Constitution of 1879 (our present Constitution) did not inaugurate wholesale reform. It incorporated just enough of Kearney's agenda to smother his movement, and otherwise mostly embellished the Constitution of 1849, making it more specific and detailed — actually tripling its length. Major

---

* Earlier, as King of the San Francisco Hoodlums, Kearney powerfully opposed Oriental immigration and Oriental contract labor. But he said many times that California workers should work as hard as the Chinese.

reform was not to be achieved until decades later — with Hiram Johnson and the Progressives.

Few were completely satisfied with the draft constitution. Conservatives condemned it as communistic, and workingmen were incensed by its scanty fare for labor. Strongest support was from the Grangers, who felt (mistakenly) it would mean lower freight rates and taxes. Approval was by a margin of only 11,000 of a total popular vote of 145,000.

Demand for political change diminished greatly with the return of prosperity to California in 1880. By the end of that year the Workingmen's Party had nearly disappeared.

CONSTITUTIONAL AND POLITICAL LEGACY OF HIRAM JOHNSON AND THE PROGRESSIVES

From the decline of Kearneyism until the rise in the early years of the twentieth century of the California Progressive Movement, California politics was dominated by the Southern Pacific Railroad (SP). It used its political power to control the Railroad Commission, maintain its exorbitant rate structure and its transportation monopoly, and amass for itself much of the state's resources. But following particularly abusive tactics of its political machine in the 1906 gubernatorial election, sentiment against SP quickened.

Voters struck hard at entrenched political leadership, approving overwhelmingly (in 1908) a constitutional amendment permitting the direct primary system, thus ending the convention system of nomination which had been used so successfully by SP. In

Hiram Johnson. His objectivity, however fractional, was remarkable, and he seemed to have a vision of a greater democracy.

Photograph courtesy of the California State Library

1910, they elected as Governor, Progressive Republican Hiram Johnson, who had promised to throw SP out of the Republican Party and out of California politics.

Aided by large majorities in both houses of the legislature, the Progressives set out not to institute a particular version of social and economic justice, but to make California government more democratic and efficient, itself a worthy enterprise. The fundamental framework of government in California is today the result of Progressive efforts.

Among their more consequential reforms were these: reanimating the Railroad Commission and placing every privately owned utility under its jurisdiction; writing woman suffrage into the Constitution; promoting worker's compensation; further weakening political party organizations by making local government, judicial, and school elections nonpartisan, and requiring that names of candidates for partisan offices appear on the ballot by office rather than by party blocs; extending the civil service; instituting procedures enabling voters to *recall* any elected official from office, and through *referendum* to block statutes from taking effect; and enacting conservation programs to protect the state's natural resources. Ostensibly the Progressives' most momentous reform was the institution in 1911 of direct legislation — *the initiative* — enabling the voters to initiate and enact laws or constitutional amendments, a still powerful popular tool.

But one of the principal reforms of the Progressives is hotly debated currently, a constitutionally required 2/3 vote of both houses of the Legislature to enact a state budget. Progressives required the 2/3 majority (still a constitutional requirement) because they wanted to make the budget bipartisan. But in practice this has meant perennial gridlock and, perhaps more importantly nearly always neither the Democrats nor the Republicans are responsible for what will be done, and for the funds that are spent to do it.

Unlike the working class Kearneyites, California Progressives were individualists and were mostly middle or upper economic class. While criticizing both politically organized capital and labor, they had much greater bias against organized labor. Today, Progressivism provides a base for liberalism in California.

HOW THE CALIFORNIA AND FEDERAL CONSTITUTIONAL SCHEMES CURRENTLY COINCIDE

Although the decision-making processes of the federal and California governments are mostly separate and distinct, there are significant affinities. For instance, both follow a pattern of limited representative government, a written constitution. amendment clauses, civilian supremacy. separated powers, checks and balances, a bicameral legislature, a popularly elected executive, and a bill of rights.

HOW CALIFORNIA'S CONSTITUTION AND THE U.S. CONSTITUTION DIFFER

CALIFORNIA'S CONSTITUTION

1. Unitary Form
2. Residual Powers
3. Plural Executive
4. Legislature Shares Power With Voters (Initiative and Referendum)
5. A Combination of Appointment and Election of Judges
6. Relatively Rigid and Detailed Constitution
7. Amendment Easy. Voters May Participate Directly

U.S. CONSTITUTION

1. Federal Form
2. Delegated Powers
3. Single Chief Executive
4. Congress Granted All Legislative Power
5. Judges Appointed by the President
6. Flexible Constitution Limited to Fundamentals
7. Amendment Difficult. No Direct Popular Input

HOW CALIFORNIA'S CONSTITUTION CHANGES: INFORMAL MODIFICATIONS

Like its federal counterpart, California's Constitution is modified informally by *custom* and by *interpretations* of the executive. legislative, and judicial branches.

FOUR METHODS OF FORMALLY AMENDING THE CALIFORNIA CONSTITUTION

PROPOSAL	APPROVAL
Amendment Proposed by 2/3 Vote of the Members of the Assembly and the Senate	
OR	
Amendment Proposed Through Initiative Petition Containing Signatures of Registered Voters Equal in Number to 8 Percent of All Votes Cast for All Candidates for Governor at the Preceding Gubernatorial Election	By a Majority of Voters Voting
OR	
Amendments Based on Recommendations of a Revisory Commission and Approved by 2/3 Vote of the Members of the Assembly and the Senate	
OR	
Constitutional Convention, Proposed By 2/3 Vote of Members of the Assembly and the Senate	

SOME MORE SIGNIFICANT FORMAL AMENDMENTS

Among the more significant *formal amendments* was the legislatively proposed amendment which in 1911, incorporated the initiative process into the California Constitution giving legislative power to the voters (previously an exclusive prerogative of the Legislature); a 1922 initiative amendment vested in the Governor power to construct and submit to the Legislature a budget for the entire state government and to reduce or eliminate items of appropriation (thus affecting substantially the relative potency of the Governor); a 1962 constitutional amendment specifically empowered the Legislature to propose revisions of the Constitution (previously accomplished only by constitutional convention); and Proposition 140, in 1990, limiting legislative terms may have further weakened the Legislature relative to the Governor and thus (some feel) worked a constitutional revision. However, in October of 1991, the California Supreme Court, ruling on Proposition 140, rejected the claim of a constitutional revision, holding that the essential powers of the Legislature were unaffected.

CONSTITUTION REVISION COMMISSION'S PRINCIPAL PROPOSALS*

- Candidates for Governor and Lieutenant Governor to run as a ticket (as do candidates for President and Vice President of the U.S.), thus eliminating the counterproductive political rivalry when the Governor and Lieutenant Governor belong to different parties.
- The now elective State Treasurer, State Superintendent of Public Instruction, and State Insurance Commissioner to be gubernatorial appointees (subject to legislative confirmation).
- The Governor and legislators to be subjected to monetary penalties should they not enact a state budget on time.
- A truly balanced state budget (instead of the current constitutional mandate that the Governor *submit* a balanced budget, but *not* requiring the Legislature to *enact* one).
- A *two-year* balanced state budget (instead of the current one-year budget), periodic revisions to insure balance throughout the fiscal period, and no rollovers of deficits from one year to another.
- A simple majority vote in each house to pass a state budget (instead of the current two-thirds of each house requirement — which results in perennial gridlock).
- Members of *both houses* be permitted to serve *three four year terms* (thus relaxing Prop. 140 term limits).
- Allow property tax increases (now prohibited by Prop. 13) to support local public schools, by a two-thirds vote of the local electorate, and permit a countywide sales tax increase of one half percent for public schools on endorsement by a *major · ity* of county voters (instead of the two-thirds vote required by Prop. 13).
- Provide for citizens charter commissions in each county to examine and amend overlapping and conflicting jurisdiction of counties, cities, and special districts.
- Give local governments strong new home rule powers, and new taxing powers to pay for local services.
  * The Constitution Revision Commission was composed of 23 members appointed by the Governor and the leaders of the Legislature.

CONSTITUTIONAL REVISION IN PRACTICE

The 1966 *constitutional revision* removed about 16,000 words from the Constitution (which had ballooned to more than ten times the size of the national document), provided annual general sessions of the Legislature, required the Legislature to pass conflict of interest legislation, and empowered the Governor to reorganize the executive branch. The voters rejected a yet more sweeping constitutional revision in 1968, but revisions in 1972, 1974 and 1978, though less ambitious, removed needless and obsolete language, reducing the size of the document by about one-third.

WHY NOT TODAY AN ENTIRELY NEW CALIFORNIA CONSTITUTION?

We might ask why in this age of change we do not change constitutions — write a new California constitution to replace our about 125 year-old document. In 1934, the legislature did ask the voters if they wanted to have a constitutional convention called. The majority voted "Yes." However, no convention has been called. Why? The same basic reason applies now as in the 1930's. Many features in our Constitution favor powerful groups in the state. These groups are content to see parts of the Constitution that do not interest them revised, but oppose altering or eliminating those parts they succeeded in having inserted.

Furthermore, *a convention* having, of course, full powers to draft an entirely *new constitution* could, for instance, mandate a unicameral state legislature. Its work could be approved by a *majority of the voters voting*, the California Legislature having no role in the ratification process. Little wonder the Legislature has not again asked the voters if they want a new constitution.

Part II
Civil Liberties
& Rights

2 CHAPTER

LIBERTIES AND RIGHTS (DENIALS AND EXTENSIONS) - AND SPECIAL PROBLEM OF UNDOCUMENTED MIGRANTS

The major sources of liberties and rights of Californians are the California and the U.S. constitutions, and California and federal laws (and treaties). Enforcement is by California courts and by federal courts, both of which honor U.S. Supreme Court precedents.

California courts also commonly cite in their decisions comparable clauses contained in *both* the constitutions of California and of the U.S. (e.g., those guaranteeing freedom of speech, press, assembly, and religion, and that no person be denied "equal protection of the laws"). Sometimes they give broader interpretations of those rights than does the U.S. Supreme Court.

California's Mixed Liberties And Rights Record: Denials

California's Supreme Court has often lead the nation in protecting liberties and rights within its jurisdiction. And the California Legislature has enacted civil rights laws predating similar national legislation. Still, California's rights record is mixed.

In 1850, Indians and Negroes were forbidden by law to testify against Caucasians. In 1852, the California Supreme Court banned such testimony by Chinese. In 1860, Indians, Negroes and Mongolians were banned from California's public schools. In 1879, California's Constitution forbade employment of Chinese by corporations or on public works. In 1882, Chinese were excluded from migrating to the U.S. (largely because of pressure originating in California). In 1924, the ban was extended to all Asians. (It particularly targeted Japanese — as did the 1913 California Alien Land Law, which prohibited aliens ineligible for citizenship from owning land or leasing it for more than three years).

In the depression years of the 1930s, California attempted to bar indigent people, (principally poor whites) from Oklahoma and Arkansas — refugees from the dust bowl, and the federal government deported tens of thousands of Californians of Mexican ancestry, many of them American citizens. During World War II, resident Japanese (including those who were American citizens) were forced (by federal authority) into detention camps. (Leading the campaign for internment was California Attorney General Earl Warren). In 1989, former UC Chancellor Ira Heyman admitted to extensive hindering of Asian Americans in the admissions process at UC. In 1994, Proposition 187 made undocumented immigrants ineligible for public education and other state financed services, including medical care (except emergency health care).* In 1998, Proposition 207 was passed seeking to end bilingual education in public schools. Also in 1998, the state high court ruled that a single criminal act can count as more than one crime under the

---

*Proposition 187 does *not* address border enforcement *or* prevention of the employment of undocumented immigrants. Its principal goal was to incite lawsuits which could result in overturning a 5-4 U.S. Supreme Court ruling *(Pyler v. Doe*, 1982) requiring states to educate undocumented immigrants. It was nullified by the courts (as unconstitutional).

three-strikes law.

In 2006, modern day slavery is permitted in sweatshops in California. Prosecutions are almost exclusively of *sex sweatshops*. The reason: The government gets a great deal of favorable press coverage for prosecuting sex sweatshops. It could prosecute all non-sex sweatshops (the vast majority of sweatshops). But it does not.

California's Mixed Liberties And Rights Record: Extensions

But examples of extension of rights in California also abound. California's Constitution of 1849 incorporated the entire federal Bill of Rights, forbade slavery, protected a wife's separate property, granted suffrage to adult white male citizens, and authorized the Legislature to extend the vote to Indians. And California's current Constitution has a Declaration of Rights longer than the entire U.S. Constitution.

Furthermore, California's Legislature was the first state legislature to furnish financial indemnity to victims of violent crime. It was also in the vanguard in enacting open housing legislation. It extended the Unruh Civil Rights Act (1959) — which prohibited discrimination by businesses selling or leasing real estate — to cover certain residential housing, and enacted the 1963 Rumford Act, which prohibited discrimination in the sale or rental of most California real estate. (Rumford predated the federal Open Housing Law by half a decade). It passed Governor Jerry Brown's Farm Labor Act which gave enforceable rights for the first time to our most downtrodden workers. California's 1967 Lanterman-Petris-Short Act (significantly amended in 2000), preventing involuntary commitment of mentally disturbed persons not deemed dangerous to themselves, was a pioneering step in the nationwide transformation of mental health laws. California also pioneered in 1975, with its so-called Inmate Bill of Rights, which guaranteed prison inmates most of the civil rights and liberties of citizens. (The scope of the law was narrowed, however, by 1994 amendments, for instance, halting government financing of inmate lawsuits challenging prison regulations).

César Chavez (1927-1993), a humble agricultural worker who by choice sustained a life of poverty, led in the 1960's, 1970's, and early 1980's, a movement of America's poorest of workers against the perennial exploitation of their labor by powerful land barons of the Southwest. It was a most unequal of contests. Yet he won.

Sacramento Bee/Dick Schmidt

But when Chavez thought to challenge the massive political-economic establishment of California in the state house, the courts, and the Agricultural Labor Relations Board, to make permanent the workers' gains and protect them (and consumers across the nation) from the birth defects and cancer many link to unregulated pesticide spraying, he and his movement were crushed.

The California courts have also pioneered the development of rights nationally. For example, in 1946 (*Mendez v. Westminster*), a federal court supported a California court in outlawing segregation of Latino students. In 1955, California's Supreme Court ruled *(People v. Caban)* evidence secured by police authorities in "unreasonable" searches not admissible in criminal trials. This was six years before *Mapp v. Ohio*, a landmark case in which the U.S. Supreme Court recognized this right. Later, in *People v. Dorado* (1965), the California Supreme Court decided that defendants must be apprised of their rights to an attorney. This was a year before the U.S. Supreme Court made this a national mandate in *Miranda v. Arizona*. In *Mulkey v. Reitman* (1966) the California Supreme Court invalidated an anti-fair fair housing initiative approved by the voters. In *Serrano v. Priest* (1977), it outlawed the method whereby California public schools were financed, ruling that it violated the "equal protection" clause of both the U.S. Constitution and the California Constitution because financing through the property tax discriminates against children living in poorer areas. It maintained its decision even after the U.S. Supreme Court stated that the U.S. Constitution said nothing concerning how public education is financed.

In 1992, Governor Wilson signed separate bills banning discrimination against gays and lesbians, and against people testing positive for the AIDS-causing HIV virus; in 1993, the Leonard Bill guaranteed "...that a student shall have the same right to exercise his or her right to free speech on campus as he or she enjoys when off campus;* in 1995, the UC Board of Regents

*The law applies to secondary schools, colleges, and universities, and is the first of its kind in the United States.

required UC to stop using "race, religion, gender, color, ethnicity or national origin" as criteria in its admissions policies (and hiring and contracting practices); in 1996 the San Francisco Board of Education eliminated a requirement at Lowell High School that Chinese American students must score higher on admission exams than must other racial and ethnic groups. In 2000, Governor Davis signed a bill to make March 31, César Chávez's birthday, a paid state holiday for state workers — the first such state holiday to honor a Latino or an organized labor leader. That same year, the Governor approved legislation which, among other things, extended civil rights protection to gays and lesbians in the areas of housing and jobs, and guaranteed their right to serve on juries. In 2001, a law was passed which granted in-state tuition to undocumented students who attended California high schools for three years and graduated. In 2002 and 2003, the Governor signed bills providing rights married couples possess to gay, lesbian, and senior partners. In 2003, Governor Davis signed legislation, authored by Senator Gil Cedillo, which would permit undocumented aliens to get driver's licenses. (He had vetoed two such bills)*. In that year he also signed a bill that provided California the strictest financial privacy laws in the nation. In 2003, he furthermore signed domestic partners legislation, which gives same-sex couples expanded rights. In 2005, Governor Schwarzenegger began emphasizing rehabilitation of imprisoned felons (instead of punishment), this hopefully to reverse a recidivism rate that is currently the highest in the nation. Also in 2005, he vetoed legislation providing for same-sex marriages. He cited an initiative constitutional amendment (Prop. 22), approved by the voters in 2000, which forbid marriage between couples of the same gender.

*Governor Schwarzenegger got the law voided; however, the legislature enacted a new law permitting undocumented to get licences. He vetoed this bill in September, 2004. Had he not vetoed, anti-licensing groups would very likely have challenged with a referendum. The voters would likely vote for repeal, thus reigniting California's racially tinged contest over Proposition 187 (which would have denied public benefits to undocumented immigrants). California permitted the uncocumenteds to secure driver's licenses for 65 years before 1953, when the legislature voted to change the law.

QUESTION OF CLOSING THE U.S. - MEXICO
BORDER TO UNDOCUMENTED

What should be done about the migration to California of undocumented aliens? We could, of course, continue with attitudes which have become a staple of American history: Exploit undocumented workers while simultaneously assailing them, focusing largely on harassing the many thousands of Mexican Indians (mostly) and Mestizos, who without documents traverse the U.S.-Mexican borderlands.

Or, we could continue the current practice of the U.S. Border Patrol, which is to police the San Diego region and three other historic points of ingress along the U.S.-Mexico border, thus forcing undocumented migrants to cross rugged mountains and hot and dry deserts (which are too vast to effectively police). This has resulted in the deaths of nearly 3,000 migrants. Between October 2004, and October 2005, 460 died. More dead bodies are probably yet to be found. This loss of life is repugnant in the highest extreme. Furthermore, the border is not secure.

There is a third option. Proposed by many Nativists, it would greatly increase border control (on the Mexican border) and expel all undocumented in the U.S. (estimated at about 10 to 11 million). Historically, such a one-sided approach has never worked. Their idea of a fence on the entire Mexican-U.S. border has drawbacks. Migrants or *coyotes* could tunnel under the fence or in other ways overcome the fence.

In recent months, with a much expanded border patrol the number of undocumented in the U.S. has *increased*. One of the reasons for this increase is that the undocumented, once they may have returned to Mexico, would have greater difficulty in crossing back to the U.S. Also, many send for their families. In addition the nativist plan does not make any reasonable proposal for replacing the workers they would deport.

In 2005, a Manhattan Institute survey found that a border enforcement only plan applied to undocumented in the U.S. is not favored by Democratic or Republican voters and though republican voters are more supportive of taking control of the border (by 58% to 33%) they also favor earned legalization of undocumented.

There is a fourth option. Theoretically, "illegals" could simply enter the U.S. legally and secure a green card.

It seems that "illegals" would prefer to enter the U.S. with documents (including a green card) rather than risk their lives in an increasingly difficult crossing, perhaps having to pay a large sum to a *coyote* (smuggler) to aid their passage, and perhaps be apprehended.

Also, many Latinos do not enter legally because the U.S. has long permitted roadblocks to documented Latino immigration. For instance, an underfinanced and lethargic bureaucracy often imposes extensive delays for applicants, causing expensive waits in hotels or motels at the border. And those who are admitted legally are often kept waiting (sometimes for years) for their green cards they need so they can function fully in our society.

There is a fifth option. If the goal is to stop undocumented entry humanely and effectively, the U.S. and Mexican governments could bring into being an inviting option for undocumented (perhaps a form of guest worker program). Fifty years ago we had such a program, the Labor Importation Program. Under the Program, workers (called *braceros* [day laborers]) were recruited in Mexico to work in the U.S. Each worker was given a six month contract by the U.S. Farm Security Administration. The F.S.A. then contracted with individual employers. After their six months tour of duty the workers were returned to Mexico.

By 1956, there were 445,000 *braceros* in the U.S., and the border was secured (see Figure 1). And while in California, in 1954, over 540,000 undocumented were apprehended, in 1956, only slightly over 23,000 were (see Figure 2).

But after 1956, *braceros* were again largely replaced in the fields by undocumented. Employers rejected the wage, minimum working and housing conditions, and duration of employment requirements of the Labor Importation Program. They used their political muscle and got termination of the Program .

With Labor Importation Program at its peak in 1956, our 1,200 member Border Patrol sealed the border.* Today, with almost eight times as much personnel, and with better surveillance equipment, it cannot (or will not). The U.S. bows to the interests of U.S. based agricultural employers; restaurateurs; building contractors; sweatshop owners; industrial employers; and employers of maids, nannies, gardeners, and the like, who engage undocumented aliens because they wish to enjoy a supply of cheap foreign labor.

---

*The U.S. secured the border (with the help of the Labor Importation Program). Much was also due to the reaction to "the red scare" of the mid 1950s. In 1954, Commissioner of Immigration Habberton said that "...about 100 present and past communists had been crossing daily into the U.S. in the El Paso area alone." *Congressional Quarterly Almanac*, Volume X. (Washington, Government Printing Office, 1954), p.170. A similar tactic is now used by many proponents of stricter border enforcement on the U.S. — Mexico border. They say that after 9/11 they feared that terrorists could enter over the unsealed border (none have been apprehended). But they do not object to the practically unguarded U.S.-Canada border [a more likely entry point for terrorists].

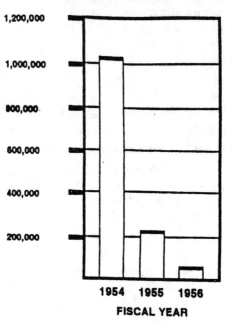

Figure 1
**APPREHENSIONS OF UNDOCUMENTED
MEXICAN ENTRANTS: 1954-1956**

FISCAL YEAR

FIGURE 2

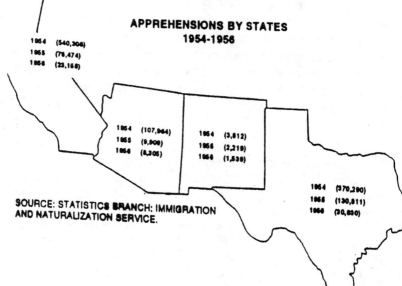

**APPREHENSIONS BY STATES
1954-1956**

1954 (540,306)
1955 (76,474)
1956 (23,168)

1954 (107,964)
1955 (9,900)
1956 (8,305)

1954 (3,812)
1955 (2,219)
1956 (1,539)

1954 (370,290)
1955 (130,811)
1956 (30,830)

SOURCE: STATISTICS BRANCH; IMMIGRATION
AND NATURALIZATION SERVICE.

There is a sixth option. We could agree with Chicano activists who remind that the Southwest of the U.S. is Mexican *irredenta* (Mexican land taken forcibly by the U.S.), reject the validity of the U.S./Mexican border, and hold that the issue of undocumented migration across it by Mexican nationals should be moot. Besides, as Fed Chairman Alan Greenspan said in 2004, we need more immigration (not less) to support our already aged population (condition worsening with the impending flood of baby boomer retirements).

The U.S. Census Bureau estimates that there are about two million undocumented immigrants in California. They come principally from Mexico,* Central America, South America, the Caribbean, Asia, and Europe. And they are not likely to leave. No previous generation of immigrants did.

---

* But the granting by a Mexican Consul of a *matricula* (consular registration) to a Mexican national abroad often serves as a substitute for amnesty. To get a *matricula* a Mexican national must produce a birth certificate and another form of identification. With this *matricula* a Mexican national without documents may get bank accounts, credit cards and credit.

Part III
Contemporary
California
Politics

3 CHAPTER
Demographic, Economic, Geographic and National Aspects

Demographic Aspects

California's population has grown enormously since 1981, up from about 23,500,000 to about 36,800,000 in 2005. It is the most populous and fastest growing American state. Accounting for much of this boom are immigrants, about five-sixths coming from other nations, and most of these from Central America, Mexico, and from Asian countries of the Pacific Rim, a tide which has made already immigrant-rich California the most racially and culturally diverse society in the world.

As noted previously, Latinos will be the popular majority in California, probably within this decade. Today, whites (non-Latino) constitute only about 48 percent of the California population, Asians about 12 percent, blacks about 7 percent, Native Americans, Aleuts, and Eskimos about .6.

Given this ethnic mix, it might be surmised that California's politics reflects demographic diversity. But the state's politics are predominantly the domain of its white (non-Latino) population, with election campaigns primarily directed at an electorate that is mainly white middle class. The reason is simple: while whites constitute less than 50 percent of the state's population, they are nearly 75 percent of California's voters. (On the other hand, Latinos are voting in greater numbers [up from seven percent in the 1992 election, to 10 percent in the 1996 election, and to 14 percent of the electorate in 2000]). But Latino voting dropped off in 2002. In that year, white, black, and Asian rates of voting also fell.

Whites (non-Latino) are also substantially older (median age is 40.3) than are ethnics, relatively affluent, and likely to be home owners. Ethnics are young (median age of Latinos is under 24), relatively poor (Latinos are now the poorest minority.), likely to be renters, have a high birth rate, and by their numbers particularly burgeon requirements for schools, jobs, housing, roads, pollution control and other environmental protection. California also has the highest youth population of any state, and the most elderly (requiring eldercare).

The result is obvious: a California politics that is increasingly ethnic, class, and generation based. And as the age gap widens and the youthful nonwhite population continues to explode, it seems our apparently perennial problem — the underlying social struggle between those who have and those who have not — will greatly govern California's politics. *

The Impact of Geography

California is immense, stretching some 1264 miles along the Pacific coastline from the Mexican border northward to Oregon and extending 150 to 375 miles inland to neighboring Arizona and Nevada. It is bigger than England, Italy, Japan, or Poland, and save Alaska and Texas larger than any other American state. And it is advantageously located — at the juncture of North America, Latin America, and the Pacific Rim — to seize upon burgeoning international markets.

California also has the most imposing mountain range in the U.S. — the Sierra Nevada. Extending down almost two-thirds of the eastern borderlands of the state, it not only supplies most of California's water, but merging with the Coast Ranges on the west encloses its great Central Valley, the richest agricultural heartland of the U.S. (and perhaps the world), and yet another phenomenon of California — a great agricultural empire in the most

---

*Also, with Latinos, because of higher birth rates and massive undocumented immigration becoming a *popular majority* in Texas, and in California (probably in less than a decade),   and with Latinos becoming the *largest minority* in the U.S. (since 2003), and with the white (non-Latino) majority becoming by 2050, *just one minority in the U.S.*, the political equation on many issues should change.

See Jorge Ramos, *The Latin Wave.* (New York: Harper/Collins, 2004) Prologue.

urbanized American state (Figure 1).

And California's lowland coastal strip, delightfully cooled by marine breezes and stretching from the Mexican border to a few miles north of San Francisco, is home to most Californians. But, fastest growing areas are mostly inland, where the summers are hot but housing is more affordable, and in the inner cities, which are attracting foreign immigrants with limited skills. Near future boom areas — in both absolute numbers and rate of growth — should also be in the interior, in the "Inland Empire" (Riverside and San Bernardino Counties), the San Joaquin Valley, the eleven-county Sacramento area, and parts of San Diego County.

California's geography also greatly impacted its politics in other ways. The North (north of the Tehachapi Mountains) is heavily forested and relatively wet, while the South is arid. Thus, North versus South rivalry was historically endemic, and principally over water distribution (and allocation of tax funds), it was also ideological and partisan, Northern Californians tended toward liberalism and the Democratic Party, and Southern Californians toward conservatism and the Republican Party. In more recent years, interior against coastal areas rivalry often exceeded North versus South.

By 2000, the partisan split was distinctly between coastal and inland, with Democrats (for instance, strongly backing environmental measures) dominant in the coastal areas, and Republicans (for instance, strongly backing conservative stands on social issues) dominant in inland areas (See figure 2).

This coastal versus inland rivalry is over such things as freeway improvements, rail financing, expansion of air hubs, affordable housing, and land use. Geography similarly figures in rivalries between big cities and suburbs, and between rural and urban interests (increasingly over water distribution), and between both real estate developers and extractive industries and conservationists (e.g., over uses of the state's vast shoreline, great interior deserts, and mountain wildernesses).

Figure 1. California Land Forms

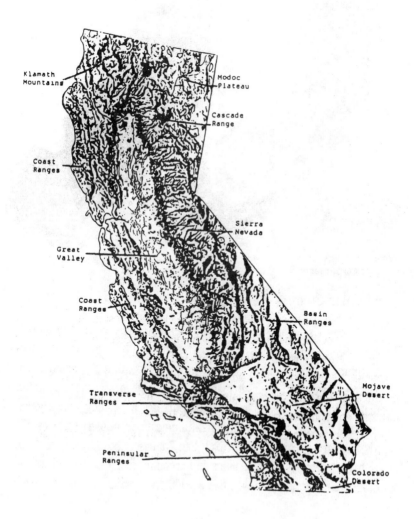

Figure 2.

Democratic   ■ **Republican**

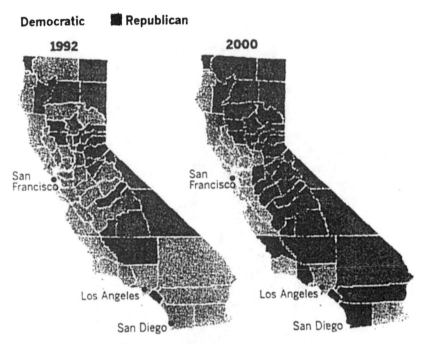

Source: *California secretary of state*.

California's Changing Economy

Today, California's economy is the eighth largest in the world (after China). Among American states it is by far the largest exporter, foremost in agriculture, aerospace, the defense industry, commercial fishing, and pop culture; second in over-all manufacturing and in commercial timber production; third in oil and mineral output; has a bustling construction industry; and is home to much of the communications industry (movies, TV, records)*. Its great seaports (principally San Francisco, Los Angeles, and San Diego) host enormous naval facilities and accommodate one-seventh of the nation's exports. Not surprisingly, these leading industries are major players in California politics.

* Currently, more Southern Californians work in multimedia than in aerospace.

THE CALIFORNIA INCOME GAP

Twenty years ago California was not a poverty state. But currently (according to the U.S. Census Bureau), the poverty rate of California is higher than the national percent, and the gap between the rich and poor continues to increase, rising faster than in the nation as a whole. Also, despite the end of the national recession in 1991, California's unemployment remains above the national average. Furthermore, most jobs created in the past six years have been poverty level. Gone are the lush days of post world war II, when California per capita income was approximately one third more than the rest of the U.S. Since the 1990s, per capita income in California have been about equal to the national average. Furthermore, the incidents of poverty is rising acutely in California, particularly among Latinos and African-Americans.

Fortunately, there are ways other than economic prosperity, though, to lift up the disadvantaged. Certain educational programs (i.e., the Cal-Grant program), more welfare reform, increase of the minimum wage,* improvement in the climate of union organization, and more low-income housing would narrow the gap.

*On January 1, 2001, the minimum wage of $6.25 per hour was raised to $6.75 at the end of 2003. The Legislature approved a bill in 2004, to increase it to $7.25 in 2005, and $7.75 in 2006, but Governor Schwarzenegger vetoed the bill. In 2005, he vetoed another bill which would have established automatic increases to keep pace with inflation. To be on a par with minimum wages of about 30 years ago would require a minimum of about $9.00.

Though California's economy has produced more millionaires than has any other state's economy, not all Californians share the wealth. There is a startling level of economic inequality in the state. Actually, California leads the nation in income inequality.

Still stressing the economy are huge budget deficits, high power costs, a state government in need of major reconstruction, high housing and insurance costs, an economic environment that often repels business and jobs, troubled schools, traffic congestion, chronic water shortages, and the smog which still blunts California's climactic advantage. Also, the states portion of military - related spending has declined from 23 percent in the 1980s to 15 percent today. Moreover, state finances have been in some disarray since the enactment in 1978 of Proposition 13 — the renowned property tax reduction initiative which has eviscerated local government finances and induced a reallotment of state revenues.

Yet, many of the Golden State's traditional advantages obtain. Tax rates, which were among the nation's highest, drifted in recent years to near the national average. The national appetite for California goods and services remains high. California exports have actually grown by more than 80 percent since 1988. And the Department of Finance indicates that California has gained substantially from the Common Market linking the U.S., Mexico, and Canada. But there is no guarantee, that any "gains" California experiences will be distributed equitably.

California's Political Prominence and National Trendsetting

California is notably prominent in the American political system. It has more votes in the national party nominating conventions than does any other state. Also, California has 55 presidential electoral votes, 21 more than the second most populous state, Texas. All of this greatly advantages California's politicians (and particularly its Governors).

California also leads all states in numbers of representatives in Congress. It was assigned 53 seats in the U.S. House by the 2002 congressional reapportionment But historically disjuncted by distinctions entailing geography and ideology, California's delegation has seldom been in agreement. Furthermore, it continues to face antagonism from other state delegations apprehensive over California's political "dominance". This opposition is completely groundless. While California's voting power in the U.S. House is based quite accurately on its current population relative to that of the other states, California is grotesquely underrepresented in the U.S. Senate. For instance, with a population of 34,501,000 in the 2000 census, it has the same vote in the Senate (2) as Wyoming, with a population of 494,000. It takes about 69 California votes to equal one Wyoming vote. Whether it is a vote on a bill, organization of the Senate, a treaty, a major federal appointment, or a proposal of a constitutional amendment, California voters are at distinct disadvantage. California is the most unrepresented state. Understandably, it is not expected that any small state will relinquish its equal representation in the Senate specifically guaranteed it in the U.S. Constitution. But California is not legitimately faulted for being

Diane Feinstein (D)   Barbara Boxer (D)

United States Senators

"politically dominant."

California's political prominence also derives from its trend setting. Californians are disposed to try the new and different to solve problems, efforts which get national attention — and frequent emulation. Initiative, referendum, and recall provisions of the California Constitution have made their way into many state Constitutions. California was the first state to pass a stiff clean water initiative (Proposition 65) and mandate clean air rules, and ideas relating to California's Proposition 13 (the property tax initiative) and its "three-strikes" legislation overspread much of the nation. Also, Proposition 187 focused national attention on immigration, as Proposition 209 did on race-and gender based affirmative action. Popular approval of term limits on California state legislators and on most other state constitutional officers in 1990 (and the California Supreme Court's decision validating these limits), boosted the term-limit movement nation-wide. And Proposition 227 (1998), requiring public school instruction in English only may influence other states, and California legislation (2002) limiting global warming (especially limiting greenhouse gases from vehicles), permitting some stem cell research, paid family leave, and privacy legislation protecting against identity theft will likely be emulated by other states.

CAL-GRANT PROGRAM--SB 1641

In 1960, California promised college access for all students with good grades, but the state never had enough money to cover all eligible. In 2000, however, Governor Davis signed a bill creating the Cal-Grant program providing scholarships for all needy students who have a C average or better.

Cal-Grant A awards are for students who have at least a B average and an annual family income of no more than :$69,600 for a family of four. They will get annual full tuition at the California State Universities or at the University of California schools, and over $10,000 yearly for private colleges.

Cal-Grant B awards are for students who have at least a C average and a maximum family income of no more than $36,300 for a family of four. They may attend a community college, and will receive $1,551 per year for books and living expenses, Should they transfer to a four-year college, full tuition plus $1,551 per year will be provided. There are also Cal-Grant scholarships for vocational training school tuition.

The Cal-Grant program is the largest aid program in the United States. Its goal is to guarantee that no student be denied a college or trade school education because of poverty. But there are possible downsides. For instance, Cal-Grants could result in more cheating and further grade inflation on the high school level, and crowding at the schools of higher education.

Cal Grant money awards do not have to be paid back. All qualified students should apply even though their family income exceeds the limits. They may be unemployed or have health problems that keep them from working when school starts. Currently, applications must be in by March 2nd.

THE ENVIRONMENT

Federal legislation, beginning in the early 1970's, shoved the environment onto the California agenda. The federal government set the national standards of water and air quality, passed a toxic substance act, created the Environmental Protection Agency, and required environmental impact statements of the effects of new developments on the environment. It left to the states responsibility for executing standards and enforcing compliance.

California, in addition to seeing to implementation of federal criteria, lead the way in areas such as water and sewage services, recycling, preservation, and waste management. It established its own Environmental Quality Act to make environmental rulings on all new projects.

During his first three years of his first term, Davis was a centrist. But in late 2002, the Governor veered to the left to defeat Bill Simon for the governorship. Then, faced with a recall election in 2003, he did his best to satisfy interests (including environmentalists).*

In late 2003, Governor Arnold Schwarzenegger propounded a new energy plan accentuating conservation, but also solar, wind, and water sources. His goal is to have 33% of the state's power generated from renewable sources by 2020.

---

* In 2002, Governor Davis signed the nation's first state legislation to combat global warming by limiting the emission of carbon dioxide and other greenhouse gases from vehicles. He sought to set an example for the rest of the country and doubtless thought to add lustre to his somewhat sullied environmental credentials. In 2003, Davis signed legislation to force industries to cease utilizing flame retardants that are contaminating people and wildlife. California was the first state to do this.

THE INFRASTRUCTURE

California's nonpartisan Legislative Analyst identifies $37.1 billion in capital investment needs. Transportation and education account for the largest proportion.

For at least the last four decades, California governors and legislators have permitted our state's infrastructure to deteriorate. This reflects to a considerable extent deliberate policy choices that favor immediate considerations over long-term investments. Also, most of the budget is dictated by law or by inescapable factuality (e.g., the Department of Prisons budget, local government needs, and welfare case loads). The $14 billion surplus in the 2000-2001 budget is why the Governor was able to award over $5 billion for transportation.

During Davis' entire first term as Governor, state spending for public kindergartens through high schools was increased by $15 billion. About $673 million was expended in 2002 alone for more health care for uninsured children, more than six times the amount allocated in Governor Wilson's last budget. The state also began a major expansion of college scholarships.

We can now expect a stinting fiscal atmosphere for infrastructural concerns for several years because of budget problems. Only when the state has sizeable surpluses does the Governor or the Legislature have a great deal of discretion. In the 1950s and 1960s California gave 15% to 20% of the general fund to the infrastructure. Its universities, water projects, roads, and parks were the envy of the other states. In 2004, next to nothing was being spent on the infrastructure — about one-fourth of one % of our general fund.

Governor Schwarzenegger has designated 2006 as a year of rebuilding, with specific emphasis on the state's infrastructure (for which he speaks of a long term $50 billion bond issue).

4 CHAPTER

CALIFORNIA'S FINANCIAL POLICIES
Governor Davis' Last Budget

After winning reelection in 2002, Governor Davis, in early 2003, at first sought to do what Governor Wilson did wih the $14.3 billion gap in the 1991-1992 budget, raise taxes and cut programs. But Democratic and Republican legislators resisted. Democrats did not want deep budget cuts. Republicans were firm in voting against any new taxes and refusing to give up previous tax cuts.

Republicans had enough votes to negate the Constitution's 2/3 majority needed to enact a state budget. Democrats in the end caved in to Republicans' "no new taxes" demand. Davis, by now facing a recall and needing a completed budget to retain his base in the Democratic party, agreed to sign the 2003-2004 budget, with its $38 billion deficit. In August, 2003, Californina had the lowest credit rating in all 50 American states. Davis was recalled in 2003.

Three Proposed Remedies to California's Fiscal Dysfunction

Recalling a governor will not solve California's fiscal crisis. And we are not going to recall legislators or Supreme Court justices. Suggested reforms, though, directed at clearing up the crises are legion. Three of the most prominent are these:

1. PROVIDING FOR NONPARTISAN REDISTRICTING

The circumstances which made the sometimes benign 2/3 rule a catastrophe this time was the *partisan reapportionment* of the Legislature in 2001. This reapportionment, making nearly all seats safely Democratic or safely Republican, virtually eliminated two-party competition, made nearly all incumbents impervious to constituent pressure, and reduced the number of compromised-minded moderates. It also enabled Democrats (sometimes aided by Republicans) to spend beyond the state's means. Finally, it permitted Republicans to block persistently new taxes

Finally, should there be redistricting of the legislature (one of the Governor's propositions)? If the long time before the voters' passage of the term limits proposition and Proposition 13 are guides, it will be some time before the voters fully understand the need for a nongerrymandered legislature.

2. ELIMINATING THE 2/3 RULE TO PASSAGE OF A BUDGET

The 2/3 rule has been in the California Constitution for more than 70 years. The fact that it can be overcome has been demonstrated many times. A legislature in a truly bipartisan mode can do so. But unfortunately in recent years, it is often overcome with

bipartisan collusion. With the latter design, Democrats have gotten Republican legislators' support for the budget by offering them billions of dollars in tax cuts and spending large amounts of money in their districts.

Some say that without the 2/3 rule we would have excessive spending. But with the 2/3 rule we had over a 40% increase in spending in the past 5 years. The 2/3 rule did not cause the budget crisis.

3. ENDING OR REDUCING TERM LIMITS

In 1990, *term limits* on legislators were constitutionally mandated by the voters to rid the Legislature of careerist politicians. The measure limited members to six years in the Assembly and eight years in the Senate. However, temed out Assembly members often win election to the Senate where they can hold a seat for eight more years, thus helping keep the Senate less affected by term limits. Still, the Legislature (mostly the Assembly) was changed.

Members are less experienced than before and lack institutional memory. With term limits, members cannot look forward to a long hereafter in their house. This makes them less likely to cooperate across party lines in exchange for future rewards. Term limits also relieve members of some responsibility for past decisions.

But many of those creating the fiscal catastrophe were among the state's most experienced politicians. Many senators had served as legislators over 10 years. Senate President *pro tem* John Burton had served in the Legislature for about 25 years. Governor Davis probably was more experienced in elective office than almost any governor.* Chief Justice Ronald George had been on the Supreme Court about 12 years.

Proposition 13

Proposition 13, the renowned property tax limitation initiative (see box), approved by the voters in 1978, remains probably the defining issue of California politics. The reason is this: The Proposition meant total revenue loss of about $340 billion from 1978 to 2005, which, coincident with California's population explosion, left the state's governments unable to fund the level of services that law and popular claims indicate. Especially hard hit were counties, cities, and school and other special districts, which depended on local property taxes. Confronted with monstrous revenue shortfalls they turned to Sacramento for operating funds, thus increasing state fiscal responsibility — and control.

There was justification for Proposition 13. Tax assessments, because of massive inflation in real estate values, had doubled and tripled in the 1970's.

But Prop. 13 created inequities, which with time deepened. Some California homeowners pay several times as much as neighbors who owned similar homes prior to Prop. 13, and start-up

*He served as chief of staff to a Governor. He was elected an Assemblyman in 1982, Controller in 1986 and in 1990, Lieutenant Governor in 1994, and Governor in 1998 and 2002.

businesses pay two or three times higher property taxes than their established competitors. Moreover, most of the tax relief goes not to homeowners, but to commercial and income property. Business property is currently reassessed less often than houses because it

---

PROPOSITION 13
(PROPERTY TAX INITIATIVE)

1. Rolled back one's property tax bill to *one percent of the property value on March 1, 1975*, with annual inflation adjustment of no more than two percent as long as the property remains under the same ownership.

2. Provided that the rate of taxation be increased only when the property is sold, at which time the increase is to *one percent of its current market value* on the change of ownership date.

3. Barred new property taxes.

4. Prohibited local governments from imposing other new taxes without a two-thirds vote of local voters. (Except that since 2000,

---

changes ownership less often.

That these inequities may be effectively addressed while also cushioning homeowners from big tax increases has been widely re-cognized. But these tidings will almost certainly be lost on the voters, two-thirds of whom are homeowners. Most oppose any tampering with the Proposition. It has become to them a symbol of social stratification and a defense of their economic security, which they feel is menaced by government, as well as by a mushrooming nonhomeowning and largely nonwhite population needing government services.

In 1992, the U.S. Supreme Court called Proposition 13

"distasteful and unwise," but nevertheless upheld its constitutionality in an 8-1 ruling. Furthermore, the California Legislature is not likely to void the popular Proposition soon, and levy higher property taxes. The political climate is no more conducive to increasing property taxes now than it was more than 28 years ago. Consequently, California's revenue from personal income taxes (a very volatile revenue source) increased from $28 billion in 1977 to $45 billion in 2000 (during the 1990's boom in the Silicon Valley) it has wavered around only $35 billion since 2002, partly causing our current fiscal crises.

GOVERNOR SCHWARZENEGGER
AND THE FISCAL CRISIS

In the 2006 fiscal year, the state will likely have a balanced budget and a small surplus (mostly because of higher state tax receipts). But nonpartisan Legislative Analyst Elizabeth Hill predicts this is just a lull, with large deficits returning in fiscal year 2007, and beyond.

In this climate, should Schwarzenegger raise taxes to cover the deficits? He promised that he would raise taxes only in an emergency. (Actually, taxes have been cut by about $12 billion in the past six years.). In one scenario, he could temporarily restore the 10% and 11% tax brackets for California's most wealthy. Governor Pete Wilson did this to reduce the state deficit a bit more than a decade ago. This tax did not seem to hurt the economy.

The Governor made a good start when he cut the auto tax and made some spending cuts, experienced a small windfall, and borrowed $15 million (approved by the voters, but probably unconstitutional). He will have to adopt deeper reductions or raise taxes to get government expenditures to equal income.

THE STATE BUDGET PROCESS

The California Budget is more than simply a fiscal document. It generally drives state policy, and its creation is the Governor's main legal responsibility. The governor has at the beginning the authority to draft a budget and at the end the item veto. It is also the legislator's most significant responsibility. The voters, through use of initiative and referendum, also have an important role.

California's Governor, unlike the President, must set out to achieve a balanced budget. But the California constitution does not require the budget *passed* by the Legislature be balanced.

Early in the budget process, the Governor outlines his budget policy. Then, state agencies make their budgetary requests, which are reviewed by the Department of Finance, acting on the Governor's behalf. In early January, he proffers to the Legislature his budget proposal, which projects both state revenues and expenditures for the fiscal year commencing July 1. His proposal is analyzed by the nonpartisan Legislative Analyst and studied by the Finance Committees in the two houses.

Differences between the houses on the Governor's proposals are reconciled in a conference committee composed of three Assembly and three Senate members. When finally considered by the Legislature, a two-thirds vote in both houses is needed for passage, a constitutional mandate that gives the minority party (or a coalition) potential power to block the budget. The Constitution requires the Legislature to approve a budget by June 15. But the deadline has seldom been met.

State Revenues

California state government gets its money from taxes, fees, bond sales, and from other levels of government. Almost 85 percent comes from the state personal income tax, sales and use taxes, bank and corporation taxes and motor vehicle fees.

Often the source of funds determines their use. For instance, restrictions usually accompany federal subventions, and much of the motor vehicle tax dollars must go for transportation, as well as road maintenance and improvements. Revenue not thus earmarked is placed in the general fund.

The single largest revenue source is the progressive personal income tax (called progressive because it schedules higher rates for higher tax brackets). Next in dollars is the sales and use tax (called regressive because it is not based on the taxpayer's ability to pay). California boasts the nation's most progressive income tax. But California's overall tax structure places a bigger burden on the poor than on the affluent.

State Expenditures

Total state government expenditures are well over $117 billion. The primary recipient is K through 12 education, which was guaranteed top spending priority by Proposition 98 (passed in 1988). Next are health and human services, a reflection of the reduced ability of local governments to raise money for education, health, and welfare through property taxes since Proposition 13. Proceeds from bond sales are spent on projects for which they are authorized. Most federal funds go for welfare grants, unemployment insurance, and education.

In 2006, Governor Schwarzenegger was speaking of long term multi-billion dollar bond issues.

REASONS PERENNIAL TRULY BALANCED STATE BUDGETS (WITHOUT TAX INCREASES) ARE DIFFICULT

As much as 70 percent of the expenditures in California budgets are mandated by voter initiatives, laws, or court orders (for such things as public health agendas, recreation and parks, specific law enforcement, and schools.). The bulk of mandated expenditures are for public schools. Proposition 98 mandates that about half of the general fund be spent for K through 12 public schools and junior colleges. (Also, law requires that some parts of the state budget get automatic revenue increases.).

5 CHAPTER

California's Strong Pressure Groups and Weak Parties

CALIFORNIA PRESSURE GROUPS

California's pressure groups, unlike California's parties are strong, and their impact is increasing. They employ nearly 2000 lobbyists, many of whom have several clients.*

Like their national counterparts, lobbyists for California pressure groups seek to influence legislatures (particularly their leaders), the executives (including bureaucrats), and the courts (especially by bringing court cases). They target the voters through TV and newspapers.

Lobbyists propose most bills introduced in the Legislature, fashion legislative stratagems, often manipulate the media, lobby on the local level, and increasingly become more powerful through use of the initiative process. They are also both sources and conduits for political contributions. The biggest spenders by far are large corporate pressure groups, all of which are represented by lobbyists in Sacramento.

With their extensive client lists and huge staffs, pressure groups are increasingly dominant. The struggle is now familiar: the concentrated power of special interests versus the largely unfocused, unrepresented, and uninformed public interest, an increasingly uneven contest.

About the current role in California government of pressure groups, Dan Walters and Jay Michael assert that "...the public face of politics — the

* Lobbyists have doubled their numbers since 1977 (the year before the anti-tax Proposition 13 centralized the financing of public schools and local governments in Sacramento).

campaigns ..., the legislative hearings, the debates on bills, the news conferences and media events — are just for show, and that lobbyists represent the real focus of the Capitol that most of the public don't even know exists."*

Arizona and Maine have systems which features nearly 100% public financing of elections, and low spending limitations. In California a similar plan may be proposed in initiative form for the 2006 ballot. Cost to California taxpayers of public financing would be about $7 a year for each eligible voter. The proposal is based on the reasoning that if the voters do not control the politicians, the special interests will.

Though business lobbies' expenditures are paramount, many organizations with strong "grass roots," for instance, "people's lobbies" such as Common Cause and the League of Women Voters, play important parts, as do issue, occupational, and various other non business groups. Instead of using money, these groups typically provide campaign volunteers to operate phone banks and to ask support by in person interviews. In any event, pressure group activity is protected by the U.S. Constitution's guarantee of freedom to petition government.

Lobbying In The Era of Proposition 140 (Term Limits)

With term limits in full sway, the influence of lobbyists is further inflated. The reasons are these: compared to the most influential lobbyists, California Assembly members restricted to six years in office, and Senators restricted to eight, possess less experience. This condition has worsened as term-limited ex-legislators have become lobbyists. A new term-limited legislator, for instance, who enter office distrusting lobbyists and resisting trafficking with them still must engage in fund-raising (for reelection campaigns) — the main interaction between legislators and lobbyists. Also term limited lead-

* Dan Walters and Jay Michael, "The Third House," California Journal, 33.2, March 2002, p. 26. Dan Walters, is a veteran Sacramento Bee columnist and Jay Michael is a long time lobbyist.

ers lack the clout they had previously to maintain order and deal with the executive branch and vested interests. Thus they are partially negated by term limits.

Finally, with term limits increasing the number of legislative races without an incumbent, special interest lobbies, in a sharp departure from past practices, have become heavily involved in financing *primary election campaigns.*

Regulation Of Pressure Groups

Lobbyists' activities in California are regulated by a 1974 reform initiative, **Proposition** 9. They must register with the Secretary of State, and both they and their employers must file public financial reports. Those not reporting face cease and desist orders or fines by the Fair Political Practices Commission, and some bad press. **Proposition** 9 has not reduced spending by pressure groups, but clearly the amount spent on legislators (limited to $10 per month per legislator) for meals and liquor is less. Other than that, and the inconvenience of reporting, lobbyists seem little hindered by the act.

A 1990 referendum (**Proposition** 112) prohibited members of the Legislature from accepting speaking fees. This law, however, left lobbyists many other ways to contribute to legislators, including, but not limited to, campaign contributions. They also can still spend on ballot issues, and on local lobbying.

One consideration that may help, although perhaps not very much, is **Proposition** 39, passed in 2000. This Proposition bans lobbyists from contributing directly to the campaigns of officials they lobby. But the proposition has been rather easily evaded. It simply makes special interests adopt different ways to finance their candidates. A favorite scheme of the special interests is to contribute to independent expenditure committees. These committees (following court rulings) are not limited.

To better control lobbyists we could pass disclosure laws to show which lobby or lobbies is paying to pass or kill laws (or effect their administration), and how nearly this spending by lobbyists interrelates with voting records and other behavior of elected officers.

PARTY AFTER THE TURN OF THE CENTURY

California's two major parties, like their national counterparts, have been weak. In California, this is by design (dating from the progressive era) and is due principally to: (1) nonpartisan local, school, and judicial elections, (2) parties with little patronage, nearly all state government jobs being covered by the civil service merit system, (3) bipartisanship, (4) cross-filing,* and (5) tradition.

Though California parties have a long practice of bipartisanship and progressivism, the parties are currently in a state of political extremism and gridlock. Probably the major reason for the current morass is the partisan redistricting of the legislature after the 2000 census. It created more partisanship by establishing "safe" districts for legislators (safely Democratic or safely Republican). With "safe" districts legislators need not reach out to new voters and other constituencies. Their base in the party is nearly all that matters to them. Ideological purity, not negotiation, is their insurance to endure in the legislature.

Currently, Democrats occupy the offices of Lieutenant Governor, all elective statewide executive offices, except Secretary of State, and nearly two-thirds of the seats in the Legislature. Registered Democrats outnumber registered Republicans by about 44% to 33%.

Most voters who are Democrats are relatively liberal, and most Republicans are relatively conservative. Some of the things California Democrats tend to support: social programs, environmental betterment, health care, business regulation, most unions, affirmative action, gay marriage, gun control, and the liberal pro-choice positions on abortion rights. California Republicans favor: law enforcement, incarceration, defense related

---

* Cross-filing is an outdated practice whereby candidates could file in the opposition party primary as well as their own.

matters, immigration control, and gun owners' rights. They oppose what they consider excess taxation. They are against affirmative action and gay marriage. They are pro-life on abortion.

Both parties present themselves as benefactors of public education. Neither wants to spend enough on the infrastructure. Most voters want more services but not more taxes.

Among ethnic groups, blacks vote about 9-1 Democratic. Whites are almost evenly divided between the major parties. Latinos and Asians vote about 2-1 Democratic. Young people, women, the middle aged, and older people all favor the Democrats, older people the least. Wealthy people vote Republican, the poor, Democratic, as does the middle class.

Californians are abandoning the major parties. Nearly 20 percent now identify as other than Democrat or Republican. Also, party labels, and "coattails" are diminishing as factors. Given these trends, voting could become yet more influenced by political advertising, personality, pressure groups, and short-term factors.

California's minor parties are even weaker. Having little chance to achieve power or even to effect the struggle between the major parties (though a minor party *may* take votes away from a major party candidate and thus affect the outcome of an election). The major parties cooperate on election laws to keep the minor parties weak.

Informal Factional Organizations Within The Parties

The vacuum resulting from weak formal party organization is partially filled in California by informal volunteer organizations (and much more by pressure groups). Most prominent of the informal organizations within the parties have been the California Republican Assembly (CRA) and the California Democratic Council (CDC). The CRA and the CDC were particularly effective in the 1940's and 1950's. In recent elections their effectiveness has diminished because of rivalry from other volunteer groups and automation of campaigns, which has lessened the need for volunteer help. A fast growing organization is the California Republican League.

Party Structure and Functions

Parties may determine their organizational structure. Each has a biennial state party convention, a state central committee, and county central committees. The *state convention* drafts a party platform and selects its slate of presidential elector candidates. The *state central committee* chooses a state chairperson and an executive committee, musters financial support and otherwise helps party candidates. (But it is too big to operate very effectively.). *County committees* — with members elected by voting party adherents — raise money, register voters, and aid candidates for the Legislature as well as the U.S. House.

Contact between California's parties and their national counterparts is limited. It is principally through California's national committee members.

6 CHAPTER
ELECTIONS

The State Primary System*

Beginning in 2002, a new legislatively created *Modified Closed Primary* provided that if you are registered to vote, *you may vote only for candidates from the party with which you are registered.* If you failed to select a political party when you registered to vote, *political parties may allow you to vote for their candidates anyway.* As previously, those candidates getting the greatest vote among their party colleagues would be on the general election ballot.

Since the redistricting after the 2000 Census made nearly of all the California legislative and U.S. House districts essentially Democratic or Republican, the real contest is in the Primaries. Here party organizations *do not* choose their own office candidates. The voters do. But since candidates appeal to the extremes in their party's base the primaries produce conservative Republican legislators and liberal democratic legislators with next to none in the middle.

As before, all voters may vote on all ballot issues and for candidates for all nonpartisan offices.

The General Election

The general election is held on the first Tuesday after the first Monday in November of even numbered years. Voters choose between candidates for partisan offices nominated in the primary, between candidates in run-off elections to nonpartisan offices, for

*Governor Schwarzenegger signed a bill returning the primary from March to June.

judicial offices, and for or against ballot propositions. In presidential election years, they also vote for California presidential electors, electors of the party getting the highest vote being elected.

Campaigns

In 1911, the Progressives transferred the focus of political campaigns from political parties to candidates and direct legislation. This has given scope to voters, but it also afforded opportunity to powerful personalities and pressure groups, with the result that expert media-oriented and strong financed campaigns and personal appeals are more significant than party.

To make up for organizational shortcomings of the parties, party candidates appoint consultants and management firms to sample voter opinion, fund raise, enlist campaign workers, advertise, and engage in numerous other campaign functions. Television, direct mail, radio, and the Internet predominate, these being the best way to touch voters. Increasingly, the Internet is used to secure campaign contributions. In statewide contests, by far the most money is spent on TV ads. Most effective, apparently are the negative ads which tend to demonize the opponent. All candidates now post web sites to give "information" and use email to correspond with followers and the media.

Restrictions enacted in 2000, limit the amount of contributions candidates can take for their election campaigns to state offices.

The California Political Practices Commission which is supposed to be a watchdog over contributions is so underfunded that it had to close 225 cases in 2005, (many of them years old) without continuing them. There are no limits at all on funds raised for or against propositions on the ballot, making proponents more dependent on special interests.

Large contributors say their donations get them *access.* Politicians agree. Experience and common sense indicate, however, that there is more than access that their money gets them.

The 2003 Recall Election

Democratic Governor Gray Davis consistently received poor public approval ratings. They plummeted during the 2001 energy crisis and never recovered. He seldom pushed policy initiatives and permitted the Legislature to set the state's agenda. He did not reveal his $38 billion budget deficit until after his 2002 election victory. Davis endorsed unpopular programs such as drivers' licenses for undocumented, and an increase in the car owners' fees by up to 300%. At no time was he able to draw even in the recall election. He lost by 55% to 45%. Gray Davis was the first Governor to be recalled in California and only the second Governor to be recalled in the U.S.

About 30% of Democratic voters voted "yes" on the recall. Men voted strongly against Davis. Women were rather evenly divided. Union members and Latinos supported Davis, but not overwhelmingly. Black and Jewish voters were Davis' chief supporters.

Republican Arnold Schwarzenegger received about 49%

of the votes cast for candidates to replace Governor Gray Davis (a winning plurality). He made a robust showing with a spectrum of voters. He got the votes of nearly 1/5 of Democratic voters, more than 40% of Independents' votes, and about 30% of the Latino vote.

Schwarzenegger ran a very disciplined campaign. He stuck to broad themes, thus avoiding alienating voters. He made these promises: to protect the people from special interests, have a fiscal overhaul, make California business friendly, help create jobs, cut motor vehicle taxes, and oppose drivers' licenses for undocumented. He promised not to raise taxes except for "an emergency." He challenged the political establishment saying often that "For the people to win, politics as usual must lose."

The 77 day recall campaign cost roughly the same amount per day as the past seven month gubernatorial campaign.

RECALL

California voters may remove any elected official. To recall an officer elected by a statewide vote, a petition containing signatures equal in number to at least twelve percent of all votes cast for all candidates for the involved office in the last election must be filed. To recall an official elected by a district of the state (e.g., state legislators or judges of the district courts of appeal), the petition must contain signatures of voters of the district equal to at least twenty percent of all votes cast for all candidates for the involved office at the last election.

The recall ballot states: "Shall (name of incumbent) be recalled ..." Those voting yes, or no, may then select from among other aspirants whose names are on the ballot. The ballot also contains a statement of charges, as well as a defense. (The incumbent need not have been charged with law violation.). If successful, he or she is reimbursed for election expenses, and is not subject to recall for at least six months.

Initiative and Referendum

In California, an initiated constitutional amendment requires a petition containing signatures of registered voters equal in number to eight percent of all votes cast for all candidates for Governor at the preceding gubernatorial election. For initiated statutes the formula is identical, except that the number of signatures required is only five percent. Initiated measures may deal with only one topic and are not subject to veto by the Governor.

Referendum is used to block a state statute from going into effect. In California, any law except an urgency measure, or one calling an election, or one providing a tax levy or an appropriation for a usual state function may be blocked. A petition must be signed by voters equal in number to at least five percent of all votes cast for all candidates for Governor in the previous gubernatorial election. A qualified petition halts enforcement of the statute until the next general election when the voters choose to approve or reject it.

State referendum is seldom used. The initiative has proved more workable.

Initiative and referendum petitions may be proffered at primary and general elections, or at special elections called by the Governor. The state Legislature, other elected officials, organized interest groups, and private citizens use them,

---

Approval of both initiatives and referendums is by a majority of voters voting.

Statewide Initiative and Referendum

Hiram Johnson and the Progressives got the devices of initiative and referendum inserted into the California Constitution in 1911. They thought this first giving of legislative power to the voters would check gridlock and special interest dominated legislatures.

But today, *most* initiatives are sponsored by special interests or by politicians; and ballot issues are qualified through the efforts of hired professional petition businesses, not by volunteers. And there still is legislative gridlock and special interest domination.

While voters complain of numerous complicated and confusing issues on their ballots, well over 60 percent of them, feeling the initiative is still a powerful popular tool, support the device.

Recent Consequential Initiatives

State Term Limits

One of the few measures which passed in the 1990 general election limited the terms of state Senators and most statewide elected executives to two terms, and Assembly members to three (Proposition 140).

Three Strikes

Proposition 187

Proposition 184, the so-called "three strikes and you're out" initiative radically increased sentences for repeat felons. The law requires sentences of 25 years to life in prison when a defendant commits a third felony. Some district attorneys, however, do not always prosecute nonviolent offenses as three-strikes cases. Also, in 2001, voters approved Proposition 36, which substituted drug treatment for prison time for many defendants who would be subject under the three-strikes law. Proposition 187 (nullified by the courts as unconstitutional) made undocumented immigrants ineligible for public education and all other state-funded services (except emergency health care). Its principal goal was to incite lawsuits which could result in overturning a 5-4 U.S. Supreme Court ruling *(Pyler v. Doe*, 1982) requiring states to educate undocumented immigrants.

The Open Primary

In the 1996 statewide primary, the voters endorsed only Proposition 198, the *Open Primary* Initiative. This statute allowed voters to traverse party lines in partisan primaries, thus giving the 12 percent of California voters registered as independents, and the increasing numbers registered as members of minor parties, an opportunity to participate in selecting the major parties' candidates. (The Proposition was declared unconstitutional by the U.S. Supreme Court in 2000.).

Affirmative Action

Marijuana for Medical Use

In the 1996 general election, California voters approved Proposition 209, which bars racial and gender preferences in government hiring, contracting, and education. (However, Proposition 209 could dispatch many programs endeavoring to assure racial equality.).

Also approved was Proposition 215, which permits use of marijuana for medical purposes (with a physician's recommendation). *

---

* On August 29, 2000, the U.S. Supreme Court barred Californians from legally giving marijuana to people who are sick and in pain.

English Instruction

Proposition 227 requires that all public school instruction be conducted in English, unless the child already knows English or would learn English faster through an alternative instruction technique.

School Property Tax Increases

Vouchers

Proposition 39 drops to 55 percent (from two-thirds) the requirement for enacting local school property tax increases. Rejected was Proposition 38, which would have established a voucher program through which parents would receive $4,000 per child from the state to pay tuition to a private school.

Before and After School Grants

Among the ballot issues, the voters approved in the 2002 general election was Proposition 49 (before and after school grants). The proposition increased state spending by up to $455 million, beginning in 2004-2005. It provided that its program grants *not* be taken from education funds guaranteed by Proposition 98.

THE PROPOSITIONS OF THE 2005 SPECIAL ELECTION

The voters voted no on all eight propositions, the four backed by the Governor (aimed, he said, at reforming California government), and the other four supported by political left and right constituencies. Apparently, the voters wanted California's problems solved by cooperation and compromise between the political branches.

This is a rather tall order given a weakened Governor who had lost his capacity to threaten to go to the ballot to gain leverage over recalcitrant legislators, (as he did to get legislators to approve workers' compensation reform). The California workers' compensation program was the worst of its kind in the U.S. There is also a gerrymandered legislature, voters who disdain deficits, borrowing, spending cuts, and tax increases. (They do want more services.)

The legislature is also deadlocked. Democratic legislators oppose program cuts, and Republican legislators reject tax increases. Furthermore, the state is required because of laws or political mandates to spend five to seven per cent more than the monies it receives.

Part IV
Principal
Decision-making
Institutions

7 CHAPTER
CALIFORNIA'S EXECUTIVE

CALIFORNIA'S EXECUTIVE

The influence of the Governor of California on the several issues Californians are now concerned about — for instance, *crime*, *immigration*, and *the economy* — is marginal. *Crime* principally reflects societal trends and demography. *Immigration* is a federal responsibility. *The economy* depends much more on the health of the national economy, federal spending, and the interest rate established as a result of Federal Reserve Board policies than on anything the Governor and legislators do. Furthermore, even in matters within the Governor's scope, legislators, lobbyists, and judges may frustrate his efforts.

Still, the Governor of California is probably second only to the President in political weight. His influence can be epic. He can animate the people of California to a compelling idea, cause, or plan which gets not only local, but also national and even international attention — and frequent emulation. Governor Hiram Johnson, for instance, ended the dominance of California by the Southern Pacific Railroad, secured the institution of the direct primary system of nomination, and the initiative process of popular legislation.

Job of Being Governor of California

The job of being Governor of California is in many respects similar to the job of being President of the U.S. (yet another reason — in addition to his being the principal executive of the largest and most influential American state — that the Governor is invariably a potential candidate for President).

Both are expected to furnish executive and administrative leadership, see that the laws are faithfully executed, originate an annual budget, recommend legislation, veto "ill advised" bills, appoint top administrative and judicial officials, lead their party, perform ceremonial functions, exercise clemency, and serve as commander in chief of the military. Both are elected to four years terms and are limited to two full terms.*

There are, however, differences in the offices. For instance, while the President appoints and removes the top federal administrative officers, California, like most states, has a "plural executive" in which several statewide executives are popularly elected and have independent constitutional powers. Also, the Governor has the item veto. The President does not.

Governor Edmund G. (Pat) Brown pushed through a mammoth state water project, an extensive highway system, and a scheme of higher education — all part of an infrastructure which laid the base for years of economic prosperity in California.

* Prop. 140, November, 1990, so limits the Governor (and most elected state executives). Only one California Governor (Earl Warren) served more than two terms.

ARCHITECT OF THE STATE BUDGET

Creation of a state budget is by far the most important work of the Governor. It is discussed in Chapter Four. Below are some of his other important powers.

Governor as Chief of State

The Governor's role as chief of a non-sovereign state is more modest than the President's nationally. Still, he makes the most of this ceremonial role because it permits him to appear as a representative of all the people of the state and provides favorable contacts with constituents.

Chief of Party

Unlike governors of some smaller states, where a U.S. Senator, or a big city mayor may have more influence, or (his) party may be fragmented into local coteries more interested in local candidates, California's Governor (like the President) is the undoubted leader of his party.

Chief Legislator

California's Governor substantially influences the legislative product by his formal authority to (1) submit the state budget, (2) call the Legislature into special session (thus keeping legislators from ignoring his legislative program), (3) address the Legislature, (4) send messages recommending legislation and policies, (5) veto bills, and (6) use his item veto to strike out or reduce items of appropriations bills.

The Governor exercises the general veto several times as

often as does the President, and while the Governor's vetoes (like the President's) may be overridden (by an absolute two-thirds vote of each legislative house), they rarely are.

Commander in Chief

The Governor heads the state militia (the National Guard), except when the President calls it into national service. Direct administration is by the Adjutant General, appointed by the Governor and approved by the President.

Generally, the Governor will use the Guard when state and local authorities cannot cope with situations, for instance, to quell riots or strikes, or deal with natural disasters such as fires, earthquakes, or floods. The Governor seldom calls on it unless requested by local authorities.

Judicial Officer

Like the President, the Governor, when making judicial appointments can substantially shape the judiciary in accordance with his views. Also like the President, he may grant clemency (pardons, reprieves, or commutations of sentences) to a person convicted of a felony. Though advised by the Adult Authority and the Board of Trustees of the California Institute for Women, the final decision is his (except he may not extend clemency in cases of impeachment, nor pardon a felon twice convicted of felonies except with approval of California's Supreme Court).

Chief Executive

Though the Governor's power of appointment is much less than the President's, his powers are substantial. He appoints (with the State Senate's approval) the Director of Finance, courts of appeal judges and Supreme Court Justices, the secretaries of principal administrative agencies, and about 100 members of various independent boards and commissions. He appoints his staff (in 2005, over 85 persons).

The Governor may also appoint U.S. Senators, state executive officers, and state judges, when vacancies occur because of disability, death, resignation, or conviction of crime. He may appoint to other state offices when no provision has been made for selection.

The Governor's Qualifications and Perquisites

The Governor must be a voter, a U.S. Citizen, and five years a California resident. He is paid $175,000 per year in 2005,* gets an allowance for a rented home, an expense account for running his office, a chauffeured automobile, and a "contingency" expense allowance.

*By way of comparison, Los Angeles Sheriff Lee Baca is paid more than $350,000 a year salary and retirement (not including other benefits). This made him the highest paid elected official in the United States. Other local salaries of California officials are similarly bloated.

The President is paid only $400,000, up from just $200,000 in 2000. Governor Schwarzenegger does not accept his $175,000-a-year salary.

The Lieutenant Governor

The Lieutenant Governor (Cruz Bustamante, Democrat, elected 1998 and 2002) succeeds to the *office* of Governor should the Governor not be able to finish his term, exercises the *power* of Governor when the Governor is incapacitated or is absent from the state, and is a member of several state boards and commissions. He is President of the Senate and may vote to break a tie. While the President and Vice-President are always of the same party, this is not true of the Governor and Lieutenant Governor. He is elected separately from the Governor and is independent of him.

Other Elected Statewide Officials

The *Attorney General* (Bill Lockyer, Democrat, elected 1998 and 2002) is the head of the Justice Department, the state's chief law enforcement officer and legal advisor to state agencies, and after the Governor, the most important state executive. He gives advisory opinions on the constitutionality of state laws and local ordinances. The office is particularly attractive since it has proved a prime path to the governorship. Governors Edmund G. (Pat) Brown, Earl Warren, and George Deukmejian previously served as Attorney General.

The *Secretary of State* (Kevin Shelley, Democrat, elected

2002) resigned in 2005, when faced by multiple investigation of his political, money raising and administrative behavior. The governor appointed former Republican state senator Bruce McPheron to complete Shelley's term. The Secretary of State is the state's elections officer and chief clerk, maintains the state's official records, accepts lobbyists' registrations and reports, and collects fees for incorporations.

The *Treasurer* (Phil Angelides, Democrat, elected 1998 and 2002) provides all custodial banking services for the state government and sees to the investment of securities.

The *Controller* (Steve Westly, Democrat, elected 2002) is the state's chief disbursing and accounting official, administers a number of state taxes, and publishes statistics on local government.

The *Insurance Commissioner* (John Garamendi, Democrat, elected for one term in 1990, and for another in 2002) oversees the operations of the Department of Insurance and may approve or disapprove many kinds of insurance rates.

The *Superintendent of Public Instruction* (John O'Connell, elected 2002), puts into force policies of the State Board of Education and is head of the Department of Education. The Superintendent is elected as a nonpartisan.

The *State Board of Equalization*, composed of the State Controller and four members elected by district, collects sales and other taxes, assesses the property of public utilities, and aids local assessors.

Managing the Bureaucracy

All executive departments except two (Justice and Education) are accountable to the Governor. Also, he may reorganize the administrative agencies (though subject to legislative veto). He is greatly assisted in managing the bureaucracy by the Department of Finance, which suggests fiscal policy, prepares the state budget, and oversees all financial activities of the state. Still, important boards and commissions are independent of him, and members' terms overlap his, thus diluting his appointment power. An example is the Public Utilities Commission.

The State Civil Service

California state employees, numbering more than 250,000 in 2005, are nearly all employed under the **merit system**. An aspect of California government employment since 1934, it features hiring and promotion on the basis of job skills, experience, and education, and protection from arbitrary dismissal and political pressure.

California's merit system has had some exceptions. **Collective bargaining agreements** set wages, benefits, and working conditions, and some work is **contracted out** to private employers who are not covered by the merit system. Furthermore, under **affirmative action** programs, historically underrepresented groups — e.g., blacks, Latinos, and women — have been hired and promoted over white males (classified as an "unprotected minority") who test higher, and during layoffs have been retained over white males with longer seniority. Latinos, Native Americans and the disabled are still underrepresented. (Latinos as a group are lowest paid.).

In June, 1995, Governor Pete Wilson, citing a series of U.S. Supreme Court rulings greatly checking the extent which race can be used as a factor in government state affirmative action programs issued an executive order designed to dismantle affirmative action. In 1996, Proposition 209 eliminated state and local affirmative action programs.

Figure 1. California's Governors

	Party	Inaugurated
Peter H. Burnett	Independent	1849
John McDougal	Independent	1851
John Bigler	Democrat	1852
John Bigler	Democrat	1854
J. Neeley Johnson	American	1856
John B. Weller	Democrat	1858
Milton S. Latham	Lecompton Democrat	1860
John G. Downey	Lecompton Democrat	1860
Leland Stanford	Republican	1862
Frederick F. Low	Union	1863
Henry H. Haight	Democrat	1867
Newton Booth	Republican	1871
Romualdo Pacheco	Republican	1875
William Irwin	Democrat	1875
George C. Perkins	Republican	1880
George Stoneman	Democrat	1883
Washington Bartlett	Democrat	1887
Robert W. Waterman	Republican	1887
Henry H. Markham	Republican	1891
James H. Budd	Democrat	1895
Henry T. Gage	Republican	1899
George C. Pardee	Republican	1903
James N. Gillett	Republican	1907
Hiram W. Johnson	Republican	1911
Hiram W. Johnson	Progressive	1915
William D. Stephens	Republican	1917
William D. Stephens	Republican	1919
Friend Wm. Richardson	Republican	1923
C.C. Young	Republican	1927
James Rolph, Jr.	Republican	1931
Frank F. Merriam	Republican	1934
Frank F. Merriam	Republican	1935
Culbert L. Olson	Democrat	1939
Earl Warren	Republican	1943
Earl Warren	Rep.-Dem.	1947
Earl Warren	Republican	1951
Goodwin J. Knight	Republican	1953
Goodwin J. Knight	Republican	1955
Edmund G. "Pat" Brown	Democrat	1959
Edmund G. "Pat" Brown	Democrat	1963
Ronald Reagan	Republican	1967
Ronald Reagan	Republican	1971
Edmund G. "Jerry" Brown	Democrat	1975
Edmund G. "Jerry" Brown	Democrat	1979
George Deukmejian	Republican	1983
George Deukmejian	Republican	1987
Pete Wilson	Republican	1991
Pete Wilson	Republican	1995
Gray Davis	Democrat	1999
Gray Davis	Democrat	2003
	(recalled in October, 2003)	
Arnold Schwarzenegger	Republican	2003

8 CHAPTER

THE CALIFORNIA LEGISLATURE

Like Congress and the legislatures of all American states except Nebraska, California's legislature is bicameral (two houses). Its Assembly, the lower house, has 80 members elected for two-year terms, and its Senate, the upper house, has 40 members elected for four-year terms. All are selected in even numbered years, except that vacancies are filled in special elections called by the Governor. State budget making is the chief constitutional function of the legislature.

Houses of Unrepresentatives Still *

The membership of California's legislature still does not mirror the state's demographics. For instance, businesspeople predominate, lawyers, while well represented, are declining in numbers. About 75 percent are white, though whites comprise less than 50 percent of the state's population. Fewer blacks (only about 5 % of the Legislature) have been elected in recent years. Latinos and Asians are grossly underrepresented, Asians the most. Only about 30 percent of the legislators are female. None are poor.

*From 1926 to 1965, California had a so called a *federal plan*. It provided that representation in California's upper house (Senate) be based on 40 geographic districts, and that no district could have more than one Senate seat. Los Angeles County was most disadvantaged. In 1965, the about 6,820,000 people of Los Angeles County had only one Senator, while the fewer than 15,000 residents of District 28 (Alpine, Inyo, and Mono Counties) also had one Senator. Northern California, which had the majority of counties but not people, controlled the Senate. Finally, after almost 40 years the U.S. Supreme Court rejected the federal plan (effective in 1965). See Jack Carney, *et al, Governments of the United States and of California*. (Dubuque, Iowa: Wm. Brown Company, 1965) pp. 223,227.

Reshaping the Legislature: Redistricting

Every ten years (following the national decennial census) the California legislature is to redraw district boundaries to reflect population changes. The Governor can approve or disapprove. Should the legislature and the Governor fail to agree, the matter goes to the State Supreme Court for resolution.

In 1981, a new and highly partisan reapportionment plan devised by the Democratic majority in the legislature (and signed by the Democratic Governor Jerry Brown, one day before he left office) gave Democrats dominance for a full decade in both the legislature and in California's U.S. House delegation. Though the Democrats still controlled the legislature in 1991, in attempting to redistrict during that year they had to contend with Republican Governor Pete Wilson and a state Supreme Court dominated by Republican appointees. Wilson vetoed the Democratic plans, calling them attempts to perpetuate Democratic control, and asking the state high court to draw the new lines. The new districts made no allowance for incumbency or politics and closely reflected population shifts. They signaled massive transfers of political power — to ethnic minorities, most particularly Latinos.

By increasing their majorities in the state Assembly and Senate in 1998, and 2000, and with a Democratic Governor, Democrats were assured of controlling the 2000 census redistricting. But in an uncommon bipartisan collaboration, state legislators attempted to make all districts safely Democratic or safely Republican.

Allowing legislators to draw their own district lines is the greatest conflict of interest in California government. In a democracy no seat should be safe for any party.

Reshaping the Legislature: Term Limits Reform

In November, 1990, California voters struck hard at state politicians by enacting Proposition 140, which limited Assembly members to a maximum of six years in office, and State Senators, the Governor, and most other constitutional officers to eight years, counting from 1991. The vote was clearly against careerist politicians and for a new class of leaders devoted (hopefully) to the true interests of constituents. It resulted in a membership which is much more diverse in race and gender (but not class). Voting 6-1 to uphold the Proposition, the State Supreme Court cleared the way for California to have an all-new legislature by 1999, one more representative of the ethnic and racial diversity in California, and with more women, business people, and professionals. In 2002, the voters (Prop. 45) chose against a return to careerism of prior Proposition 140 days.

Reshaping the Legislature:
Behavior Modification

Term limits on California state legislators is the towering reform of the present generation of reforms in California. It issued, as had Proposition 112 (in 1990, outlawing honoraria), from public disgust with the legislature in general, and specifically with improper influence of single interest groups over legislators.

Prop. 112 bans honoraria, strictly limits gifts, installs stricter ethical guidelines, and requires legislators to take a class on ethics every year. Members are also barred from voting on matters in which they have a personal financial interest. There are also strict limits on speaking fees. But they are not restricted from earning outside income. The monumental Prop. 140 limits legislator's terms. But these merely put strictures on *individual legislators* yet leave the system itself intact. It seems that not until election campaign spending is effectively limited, and legislative elections are substantially publicly financed, will the views of the voters, not just those of major contributors, be effectively represented.

Assembly Leaders

The *Speaker of the Assembly* is chosen for the post by members of his chamber, and is the most powerful officer in the legislature. Except for the Governor, he or she is probably the most influential official in the state. The Speaker's important powers as presiding officer include:

1. Appointing the chair, vice-chair, and members of all other Assembly committees (except the Rules Committee);*
2. interpreting the rules and deciding on points of order;
3. recognizing members who wish to speak; and
4. serving as an ex-*officio* member of all committees.

His position as speaker also enables him to raise large sums of campaign money, a role which enhances his speakership.

Other important Assembly officers are the Speaker *pro-tempore*, and the *majority* and *minority floor leaders*. The *Speaker pro tempore* is elected by the Assembly to preside in the absence of the Speaker. The *majority floor leader* is selected by the Speaker, and is his personal representative on the floor. A *minority floor leader*, customarily elected by the caucus of the minority party, leads the opposition party in the Assembly.

Senate Leaders

Like the Vice President on the federal level, the *Lieutenant Governor* presides over the upper house (but usually does not attend). He may not introduce a bill, nor vote except in the event of a tie vote.

The President *pro tempore*, elected to the post by members of the Senate, presides when the Lieutenant Governor is absent, is the most influential Senator, and retains at all times his speaking, voting, and other rights as a Senator. He is also majority floor leader, heads the important Rules Committee (which appoints all committees) and chooses each committee chair, has general responsibility for the administrative functions of the Senate, and oversees the work of the interim committees.

---

* He appoints five of the eight members of the Rules Committee (and its chair).

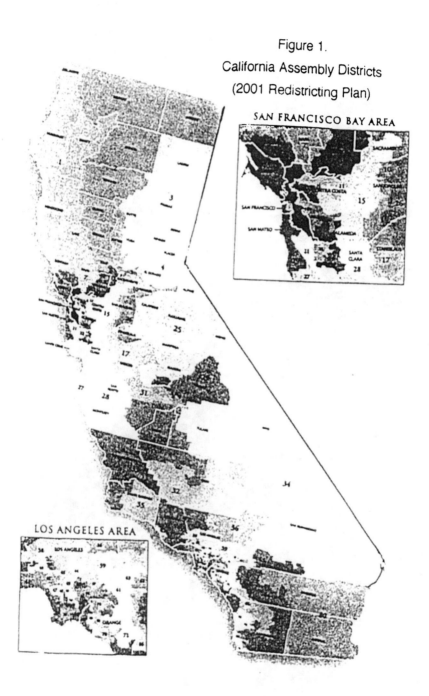

Figure 1.
California Assembly Districts
(2001 Redistricting Plan)

SAN FRANCISCO BAY AREA

LOS ANGELES AREA

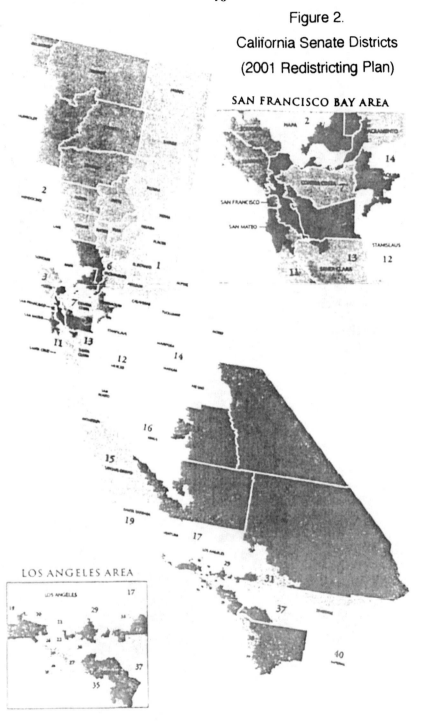

Figure 2.
California Senate Districts
(2001 Redistricting Plan)

LAW-MAKING

INTRODUCTION OF BILLS

Only a member of the Legislature may introduce bills. Most *originate* with the Governor, departments and agencies of the executive branch, or pressure groups. A bill is introduced by a member submitting a signed copy to the clerk of the chamber of which he belongs. After being numbered, it is assigned by the Rules Committee to an appropriate committee. About 5,000 bills are introduced in the two-year period.

Consideration by Committees

The crucial stage for most bills is in the standing (or policy) committee. If the bill is important, the committee holds public hearings, welcomes testimony, and may subpoena both witnesses and documents. All sessions are open unless by two-thirds vote the legislature rules a particular session be closed.

A committee may: (1) report the bill out with the recommendation "do pass" (with or without proposing amendments); (2) report it out without recommendation; or (3) table it. About one-half are tabled (or pigeonholed). A majority of the members of a chamber can force a bill out of committee, but this process is seldom used.

THE LEGISLATURE'S NONLEGISLATIVE FUNCTIONS

1. Create administrative departments and agencies, define their activities, appropriate funds for their operation, and frequently to specify their organization and procedures.
2. Participate in amending the California and the U.S. Constitution.
3. Impeach and remove elective state officers and judges, employing procedures similar to those used by Congress on the federal level. (A resolution to impeach must be approved in the Assembly by majority vote. The Senate tries the case, concurrence of two-thirds of its total membership being required for conviction.) An officer found guilty is removed from office. Only one has been convicted in impeachment proceedings.
4. Investigate under either single-house or concurrent resolution. Most investigations take place between sessions by committees called interim committees.
5. Consider (by the Senate) appointments proposed by the Governor.

Consideration by the Two Houses

Bills are debated in the order in which they are reported by committees. Debate may be ended by majority vote and the question brought to a vote.

Thus, unlike in the U.S. Senate, there are no minority filibusters in either house of California's legislature. Also, unlike in Congress, the final vote on all bills is by roll call. Furthermore, passage requires (unlike in Congress) a majority vote of the **entire** membership.*

If the second house passes the bill in a form different from the version of the house where it originated, it must be sent back. If the two houses cannot agree on its provisions, a **conference committee** composed of three Assemblymen appointed by the Speaker, and three Senators appointed by the Committee on Rules, meets to iron out the differences. If the committee report is not accepted by both houses, a new conference committee is appointed. If after three conference committees on any bill, the houses still disagree, the bill is killed.

Action by the Governor

A bill approved by the two houses and signed by their presiding officers is sent to the Governor. If he signs, it becomes law and goes into effect on January 1 "... next following a 90-day period from the date of enactment of the statute..."[2] except statutes calling elections, or providing tax levies or appropriations for usual state expenditures — which become effective immediately on the Governor's signature.

If the Governor does not sign the bill within twelve days and the legislature is still in session, it becomes law without his signature. The Governor may also veto the bill, returning it to the house where it originated, with a statement of his objections, or he may "item" veto to reduce or eliminate any item in an appropriation bill. The Governor's vetoes may be overridden, but only by a vote of two-thirds of the members of each house.**

* Constitutional amendments and bond measures proposed to the people must have a 2/3 majority vote in both houses (2/3 of the total membership, that is). They must receive majority votes of the voters.

**Bond issues and constitutional amendments are not submitted to the Governor.

QUALIFICATIONS, SALARIES, AND PERQUISITES

A legislator must be at least eighteen years old, a citizen and inhabitant of the state three years and for one year prior to the election a resident of the district for which elected.

Senators and Assembly members are paid an annual salary of $110,800 (highest in the United States), set by an independent Citizens Compensation Commission. They also receive a tax free per diem living expense allowance of $163 while the Legislature is in session (including weekends), participate in a contributory retirement plan, and receive free gasoline for a leased automobile, and secretarial and telephone allowances. Actually, with per diem and other perquisites, they effectively receive more income than members of Congress.

Members are privileged from arrest, except for treason, felony, or breach of peace, and are not subject to civil process during a session and for fifteen days before and after.

SESSIONS

Like Congress, California's Legislature meets in annual general sessions, and in special (or extraordinary) sessions.

From 1946 to 1967, it met in general session only in odd-numbered years and then only for 120 working days. Under the late Democratic Speaker, Jesse Unruh, the Constitution was amended (1966) to provide for annual general sessions, and the Legislature became a full time professional body. This initiated a nationwide trend.

General sessions begin on Monday after the first day in January and are of indefinite duration. Like Congress, the California Legislature may terminate its annual sessions whenever it chooses.

The Legislature may also be called by the Governor into special session at any time. He lists the subjects to be considered, and may add additional items, and the Legislature may legislate only on subjects he lists. Special sessions are between regular sessions or are concurrent.

WILLIE BROWN JR. Like the illustrious Speaker Jesse Unruh before him, he rose from abysmal poverty in his native Texas to prominence in California as a populist state Assemblyman with a focus on civil rights.

Elected Speaker of the Assembly in 1980, a brilliant strategist and manipulator, Brown held that post longer than any predecessor (14 years). He also became one of the nation's most influential African-American political personages, and after the Governor, the most powerful political figure in California.

But Willie Brown accumulated considerable enmity. This figured prominently in popular support for the term limit Proposition 140.

9 CHAPTER
CALIFORNIA'S JUDICIAL PROCESS

California courts, like federal courts, observe the U.S. Constitution, federal statutes, and treaties even if they conflict with California's Constitution or laws. But they are not subservient to federal courts. They are separate and distinct. And they hear the great preponderance of criminal cases and civil disputes in California, applying statute law, common law, and equity, with as much finality as if there were no federal courts.

The Supreme Court and the Current Political and Fiscal Crisis

Most Americans think, incorrectly, that the Supreme Court is not political. It is. The Court, for instance, intruded into the recent political and fiscal catastrophes by both its action and inaction. *First,* it frustrated the voters' opportunity to vote on a nonpartisan commission to reapportion the legislature. The court mysteriously ruled a proposed initiative to do this (Proposition 26) unconstitutional for containing two subjects. The Court never before dispatched other multiple subjects initiatives from the ballot. There were several.

Second, it ignored the Constitution's framers' attempts to limit borrowing. The Constitution (Article XVI) requires that any borrowing not "...exceed the sum of three hundred thousand dollars ($300,000)..." unless it is for a "single object of work." This means it must be for lasting public improvements, such as for bridges, roads, or schools, *not for the everyday cost of government.* In other words, it forbids borrowing for payment for past operating deficits. The Court failed to enforce the Constitution's limitations on borrowing.

Judicial Policy Making

California's judiciary is possibly the most powerful branch of California's government. The reason is this: in addition to being involved in adjudication, law enforcement, and specialized activities (probate, divorce, suits for damages, etc.), California courts are often dominant in political decision making.

The State Supreme Court interprets the many clauses of California's extremely detailed Constitution, and has the power — which it has not hesitated to employ — to void acts of the legislature and initiatives enacted by the voters which it says conflict with it (or the U.S. Constitution). California courts also interpret California laws and sometimes dictate new meanings to statutes and to the Constitution. And though California legislators shape legislative districts, California courts supervise this function. They also decide if laws are unreasonable or arbitrary, if local officials are complying with the law, or if the Governor is exceeding his powers.

California's Supreme Court has won much praise for excellence and independence, and for leadership of its forceful Chief Justices. Under Phil Gibson, Roger Traynor, and Donald Wright, it often showed the way for the U.S. Supreme Court, and both the Bird and Tobriner Courts were activist. Most of the landmarks of the law during their tenure resulted from judicial activism, which often asserted a doctrine of "independent state grounds" to provide individual rights beyond those mandated under the U.S. Constitution.

But with the liberal-activist majority replaced by more cautious and more conservative Justices now led by Chief Justice George, many see little prospect for much activism, but instead expect the Court to continue to look for guidance to the U.S. Supreme Court, and to defer to the legislature and the Governor.

Though most of the Justices were appointed by rather conservative Republican Governors, California Supreme Court rulings such as the 1996 decisions permitting limited exceptions to the "three-strikes-and-you're-out" law, and decisions making it easier for some battered women to prove they killed in self-defense and win acquittals,* indicate that the Court may not be so easily categorized. Overall, though, they tend to be pro-business and pro-prosecution (in criminal cases).

STRUCTURE OF CALIFORNIA'S JUDICIARY

California has three types of courts: trial courts, courts of appeal, and a Supreme Court.

Trial Courts

Trial courts consider all felony trials, juvenile criminal cases, domestic relations matters, probate of wills, and civil cases. They also decide civil claims cases involving $25,000 or less, and minor criminal offenses (misdemeanors and infractions). They issue arrest warrants for persons charged with serious crimes, and hold preliminary hearings for suspects (18 or over) later bound over to a prosecutor or grand jury for possible trial. Very large counties have specialized divisions. Appeals go directly to the Supreme Court if the death penalty is involved, otherwise they go to a court of appeal.

Courts of Appeal

There are six courts of appeal districts (Los Angeles, San Francisco, San Diego, Sacramento, San Jose and Fresno). Three judges sit on a case, and decisions are by majority vote. Juries are not employed since questions of law, and not of fact, are usually involved.

Courts of appeal have no original jurisdiction. They hear only appeals from trial court actions, and decisions of quasi-judicial boards and commissions. Appeal from their decisions is to the Supreme Court (if it accepts the appeal). Most cases get no higher than the court of appeal.

---

*In 2004, Governor Schwarzenegger went further. He signed a bill which provided the prisoners convicted of crimes before expert testimony about battered women's syndrome was permitted in court could bring such evidence in efforts to get their sentences reduced or their convictions reversed.

The State Supreme Court

The **State Supreme Court** has a Chief Justice and six Associate Justices. Except for issuing writs, its work consists almost entirely of deciding appeals on questions of law from lower state courts and reviewing orders of the Public Utilities Commission. It generally hears only about five percent of these appeals. The Supreme Court must review all cases entailing the death penalty. The Court has original jurisdiction to issue writs of prohibition (to keep a lower court from asserting jurisdiction over a case), **mandamus** (to force an officer to act in accord with legal obligations), and **habeas corpus** (a court order directing an official who has an individual in custody to bring his prisoner to court and there demonstrate cause for the detention). Decision is by majority vote, and is final unless there is a possible conflict between state law (or its interpretation) and the U.S. Constitution or federal law. The U.S. Supreme Court, but no lower federal court, reviews its decisions.

How Judges Are Selected*

Trial court judges are elected by district to six-year terms. Elections are generally not hotly contested. Vacancies on the bench in these courts are filled by the Governor.

Courts of appeal judges and Supreme Court Justices are initially appointed by the Governor with the approval of the **Commission on Judicial Appointments.** After appointment, their names go on the ballot for confirmation at the next gubernatorial election, and again for retention upon expiration of the term they are filling. Then after another twelve years in office, the particular judge must face popular election to decide if he or she may continue in office. The ballot contains the incumbent's name, without opponents.

Until 1986, no Supreme Court Justice (or court of appeal judge) failed to receive a majority of "yes" votes. In the 1986 gen-

---

*To be a judge in any California court, a person must be a practicing attorney in California.

Chief Justice Ronald George

eral election, however, Chief Justice Rose Bird and Justices Cruz Reynoso and Joseph Grodin lost in their re-election bids, thus ending a 30 year liberal domination of the Court. The principal voter complaint was that they (and particularly Bird) were "soft on crime" and specifically were responsible for the Court's failure to order an execution of any death penalty during Rose Bird's tenure. Currently, the Court has a solid conservative majority.

How Judges Are Disciplined and Removed

The Supreme Court may discipline or remove a judge (or a commissioner or a referee) upon recommendation of the *Commission of Judicial Performance.* (This is seldom done.) Any judge found guilty of a felony or a crime involving moral turpitude, such conviction having been upheld by a higher court, *must* be removed by the Supreme Court.

The Supreme Court Justices themselves may be censured, removed, or retired on the basis of a recommendation by the *Commission of Judicial Performance,* approved by a tribunal of court of appeal judges selected by lot.

Judges may also be recalled or impeached.

THE JUDICIAL COUNCIL

Like most states, California has a *Judicial Council* to overlook the administration of its court system. Comprised of a board presided over by the Chief Justice, it establishes rules of court procedure and administration, advises (and at times decrees) procedural improvements, and recommends statutory and constitutional changes.

CALIFORNIA COMMON LAW, STATUTE LAW, AND EQUITY

Statute law is legislated law.

Common law is judge made law, based on the principle of stare decisis, meaning that as far as possible a case is decided on the basis of earlier similar cases. Though common law is today largely superseded by state statutes, it remains the foundation for California's legal system.

Equity supplements common law, providing substantial justice where the strict application of common law would result in injustice or hardship. Two examples would be a court order forbidding an action (e.g., a union going on strike) that would cause irreparable damage, or one requiring an act (e.g., that a person fulfill a contract). The typical remedy in statute or common law, on the other hand, is money damages awarded only after the hurt has been done and the injured party can show what he suffered.

CIVIL PROCEDURE

Civil cases involve two or more entities (private persons, businesses, or government agencies) and proceedings to enforce a right, or obtain compensation for its violation. They are distinguished from criminal cases, which involve offenses against the law of the land.

Legal action is started when an entity (the plaintiff) sues another (the defendant), before a judge alone, or by a judge and jury, a full jury of twelve (unless both plaintiff and defendant agree to fewer), a three-fourths vote being needed for a decision. There is no presumption of innocence of the defendant, who can be held liable if there is a determination of a *preponderance of evi-dence,* that is, a more than 50 percent probability of guilt. The defendant *must* testify if called. The judge may raise or lower damages awarded by the jury. The parties must abide by the court's ruling on the case or risk being held in contempt of court and liable to a fine or jail sentence. Most cases never go to full trial, but are settled out of court because this may be cheaper, more convenient, less aggravating, or quicker.

GRAND JURIES AND TRIAL JURIES

California employs the standard jury system used in the U.S. *Grand juries* of 19 citizens in most counties, nominated by county judges and chosen by lottery, investigate local agencies. They also hand down criminal indictments of suspected felons.* Proceedings are secret, and the accused may not have an attorney present, or cross-examine witnesses.

The *trial (petit)* jury makes a determination of facts, finding the accused guilty or not guilty (by unanimous vote in a criminal case). The judge decides all questions of law. The accused may waive a jury trial.

There are usually 12 citizens on a trial jury, but there may be a lesser number for a misdemeanor trial or a civil case. In a civil case three-fourths of a jury may render a verdict. Names of prospective jurors are taken from DMV records of licensed drivers and from other lists. In 2000, jurors pay was raised from $5 to $15 a day.

* The district attorney usually files an *information* against the accused instead of taking his charges to a grand jury. Only in a relatively few instances when notorious crimes are entailed or, for instance, a public official is involved, does he seek indictment.

FELONIES, MISDEMEANORS, AND INFRACTIONS IN CALIFORNIA LAW

Felonies: Serious crimes (e.g., homicide, arson, certain drug law violations, kidnapping, robbery, forgery, aggravated assault) punishable by imprisonment in a penitentiary for a year or more (or by death). A person accused of a felony is tried by a jury, but may waive it.

Misdemeanors: Less serious violations of law (e.g., driving under the influence, disorderly conduct, petty theft) punishable by a fine or sentence to the county jail (or both). They are usually tried in summary process without jury, though the defendant may plead not guilty and demand a jury trial.

Infractions: Less serious than misdemeanors, they constitute the bulk of the violations defined in the California Motor Vehicle Code. Usually the person cited simply goes to the clerk of the court and pays for the ticket though he (or the prosecutor) may ask for a court trial, where guilt or innocence is decided by the judge (or by a special commissioner in some counties), if the infraction is a traffic offense.

CRIMINAL PROCEDURE

In criminal cases, the government is always the injured party, and thus the one which initiates proceedings. When arrested by a police authority, an accused is "booked" for a named offense. If the booking is for a felony, the district attorney decides whether to file a felony charge. If so charged, the accused goes before a judge of a trial court for a preliminary hearing. If the defendant can not afford an attorney he is supplied a court- appointed attorney. Most felony defendants require court-appointed attorneys.

The judge informs the accused of his legal rights. If the accused pleads guilty, or if the judge feels the evidence warrants, he commits him to the trial court. If an information against the accused is signed by the district attorney, or the county grand jury votes a true bill of indictment, the defendant appears in superior court where he or she enters a plea,* and may opt for a jury trial. The defendant is presumed innocent until proved guilty beyond a reasonable doubt.

The district attorney presents the government's case; the counsel for the accused pleads the defense case; witnesses testify and are cross-examined; ** the defense counsel summarizes his case; and the government's attorney follows with a final argument. The judge then instructs the jury on the law applicable to the case, and the jury — by unanimous vote — must render a verdict based on the judge's instructions and the evidence. If the verdict is guilty, the presiding judge, after receiving a probation report, passes sentence according to the law — a fine, a prison term, or even death. During the interlude, the defendant's attorney may have asked for a new trial or filed for appeal.

With misdemeanors, procedures are generally simpler.

*Most cases are plea bargained, a procedure in which a lesser sentence is arranged in exchange for a guilty plea, and the trial phase is eliminated.

**The defendant does not have to testify. He or she can invoke a Fifth Amendment right against self-incrimination.

Part V
Local Government

10 CHAPTER
Local Decision-Making Institutions

Although local units of state government are not mentioned in the U.S. Constitution, California (like all American states) has created them, and in its Constitution and statutes determines their functions and organization.

THE LOOTING OF LOCAL GOVERNMENT BUDGETS

In recent years, to balance deficit encumbered budgets, the State of California has looted local government budgets. It is not that local governments are flush. They have been badly overstretched for over 27 years. Proposition 13, in 1978, deprived them of most property tax funds and provided that local tax measures must be approved by a 2/3 vote of local voters.*

Counties have been hardest hit (and thus are more dependent on the state and federal governments). Cities do not have the burden of human service programs as do the counties, have greater flexibility in raising revenue, and enjoy more political clout because their mayors are higher profile than are county officials.

Governor Gray Davis continued the practice of Governors Pete Wilson and George Deukmejian: keeping local governments from full financial independence. His 2003-2004 budget continued

---

* Since 2000, taxes needed for repairing school facilities bonds require approval by only 55% of the local voters.

Figure 1
California's 58 Counties

Source: California State Controller

the plundering. Local government budgets were reduced by about $825 million. Governor Schwarzenegger supported a constitutional amendment to prevent state looting of their funds. It passed in 2004, (Proposition 1A), amending the Constitution by limiting the state's power to raid local treasuries. However, the state is not fettered in any real emergency.

COUNTY GOVERNMENTS

There are three types of local governments in California: county, city and special district.

Counties are administrative subdivisions of the state. California has 58. The most populous (Los Angeles) has about 10 million people, the least populous (Alpine) about 1,220. The largest in area (San Bernardino) covers over 20,000 square miles, the smallest (San Francisco) fewer than 100.

Each county is required to elect a governing body — a board of supervisors, and every county must elect a sheriff, a district attorney, and an assessor. Most counties also have a chief administrative officer (appointed by the board of supervisors), a clerk, a recorder, and a legal counsel.

By far, the greatest county expenditures are for *public assistance and public safety.* The biggest revenue source is state agencies. Counties serve as agents of the state in operating health and welfare programs. But they are also local units of government in providing fire, police, courts, school districts, libraries, and other services. Inevitably, the state's priorities get precedence.

General-Law, Home Rule, and Consolidated Counties

Most California counties (46) are **general-law counties** organized under uniform laws enacted by the state Legislature.

But most large counties are **home rule**. A **home rule (charter) county** has greater flexibility in determining the number of supervisors, providing for a county-manager system of centralized administration, and combining county offices. Any California county may draft a home-rule charter (which must be approved by a majority of voters voting in a special election).

San Francisco (a charter county) is the only **consolidated city-county** in California. As the City and County of San Francisco it has one legislative arm, one police force, and one set of financial officers.

City Governments

Coming into being at the request of their residents, cities are (unlike counties) more a local unit of self-government than administrative subdivisions. They supply an extensive series of mostly *physical services* rather than social services. There were 475 of them incorporated in California in 2005 (88 of them in Los Angeles County), ranging in size from Vernon (about 100 residents) to Los Angeles (about 3.95 million).

They receive nearly three-fourths of their revenues from city taxes and service charges, and expend more for local public safety than for anything else. They receive about 15 percent of their revenues from state and federal governments.

In California, most large cities are **charter cities**.

Plans of City Government

Under the **strong-mayor plan** of city government, the

mayor is elected by the voters independently of the council, plays a major role in both policy formulation and administration, and has a veto over council ordinances. Los Angeles and San Francisco are among the few California strong-mayor cities.*

In a **strong-council plan** of the city government the **council** has primary responsibility and power of both policy-making and administration. The mayor is simply a member of the council selected by it to preside, has mostly ceremonial functions, and no veto power.

In the **council-manager plan**, a popularly elected **council** enacts ordinances, adopts the budget, and appoints the **city-manager**. The manager directs all city departments, and prepares the annual budget. He is responsible to the council and may be removed by it. The mayor presides over the city council and performs ceremonial functions is now more widely used here than in any other state.

Under the **commission plan** of city governments, popularly elected commissioners serve collectively as a legislative body and individually as heads of departments. There is no separate executive. Since Fresno dropped the form in 1959, in favor of the council-manager plan, no California city has indicated interest.

Special Districts

Special districts are the most varied and numerous of all units of government in California, ranging from large regional districts such as the Metropolitan Water District of Southern

---

* In 2004, Los Angeles City Council members are the nation's highest paid city council members.

California to local mosquito abatement districts. Their annual financial transactions exceed those of all cities and counties of the state combined.

California uses special districts on a wider scale than does any other state. School districts are the most common. Others (now totaling about 5,000) deal with matters such as water supply, sanitation, fire protection, air pollution control, flood control, irrigation, and highways — problems which are not coterminous with city and county boundaries.

They secure funds by taxing property owners within the district, by charging fees for goods or services, and from state aid.

Regional Governance

In California, nearly all important local powers (e.g., over land use) are retained by local officials. But many of California's most pressing problems, such as growth management (e.g., air quality and water and waste management), and transportation — are increasingly regional in nature. Being regional, they require regional solutions, probably through regional governance.

While there are no regional governments in California, there are a number of voluntary associations of local government agencies to deal with regional problems. Today, most areas of California are within the jurisdictions of regional agencies.*

---

* Examples are the Southern California Association of Governments (SCAG) and the Association of Bay Area Governments (ABAG).

BIBLIOGRAPHIC NOTE ON CURRENT SOURCES

We have in California a number of worthy reference sources on our state's governments and politics. *The California Political Almanac* is a remarkably comprehensive source book on California's political process, issues, and practitioners. The *California Handbook* is the standard guide to locating sources about California state and local government. *The California Roster* is also highly useful, as are *The Encyclopedia of California*, and *The California Almanac*, *The Almanac of American Politics*, *The California Statistical Abstract*, *and California Cities and Towns*.

California State Publications, issued monthly by the California State Library, Sacramento, is the most extensive list of state documents. The state's library is itself a fertile source, as is the Bancroft Library at the University of California at Berkeley, the California Historical Society's Library in San Francisco, and the Huntington Library in San Marino.

Major newspapers, and particularly the *Sacramento Bee* and the *Los Angeles Times*, feature current information and opinion on California topics. The *California Journal*, published monthly in Sacramento by the California Journal Press, is vital to staying abreast with California issues, politics, and government, and *The California Government and Politics Annual*, also published in Sacramento, is a yearly anthology of *Journal* articles.